ISBN 978-0-282-25107-9
PIBN 10573120

1 MONTH OF
FREE
READING

at
www.ForgottenBooks.com

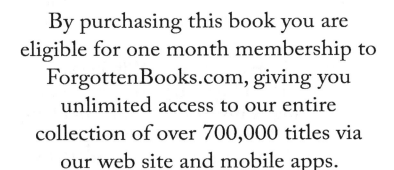

By purchasing this book you are
eligible for one month membership to
ForgottenBooks.com, giving you
unlimited access to our entire
collection of over 700,000 titles via
our web site and mobile apps.

To claim your free month visit:
www.forgottenbooks.com/free573120

English
Français
Deutsche
Italiano
Español
Português

www.forgottenbooks.com

Mythology Photography **Fiction**
Fishing Christianity **Art** Cooking
Essays Buddhism Freemasonry
Medicine **Biology** Music **Ancient**
Egypt Evolution Carpentry Physics
Dance Geology **Mathematics** Fitness
Shakespeare **Folklore** Yoga Marketing
Confidence Immortality Biographies
Poetry **Psychology** Witchcraft
Electronics Chemistry History **Law**
Accounting **Philosophy** Anthropology
Alchemy Drama Quantum Mechanics
Atheism Sexual Health **Ancient History**
Entrepreneurship Languages Sport
Paleontology Needlework Islam
Metaphysics Investment Archaeology
Parenting Statistics Criminology
Motivational

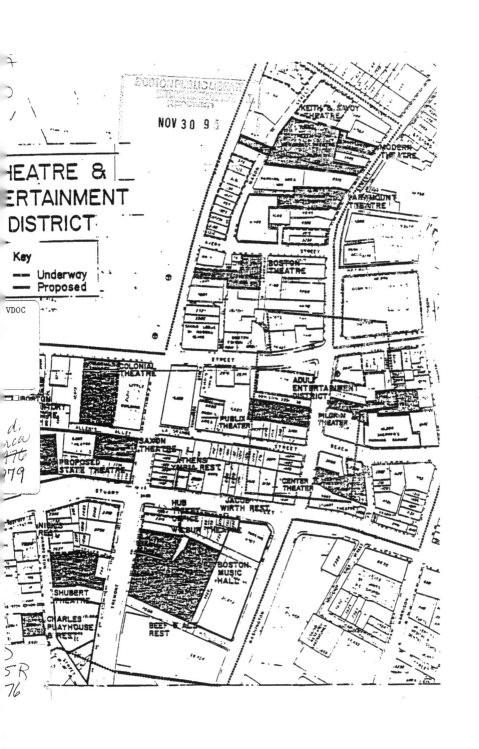

THEATRE &
ERTAINMENT
DISTRICT

Key
-- Underway
— Proposed

KEITH'S SAVOY THEATRE

MODERN THEATRE

PARAMOUNT THEATRE

BOSTON THEATRE

COLONIAL THEATRE

ADULT ENTERTAINMENT DISTRICT

PUBLIX THEATER

PILGRIM THEATER

SAXON THEATRE

PROPOSED STATE THEATRE

ATHENS OLYMPIA REST.

CENTER THEATER

HUB OFFICE

JACOB WIRTH REST.

WILBUR THEATRE

BOSTON MUSIC HALL

SHUBERT THEATRE

CHARLES PLAYHOUSE & REST.

BEEF & ALE REST.

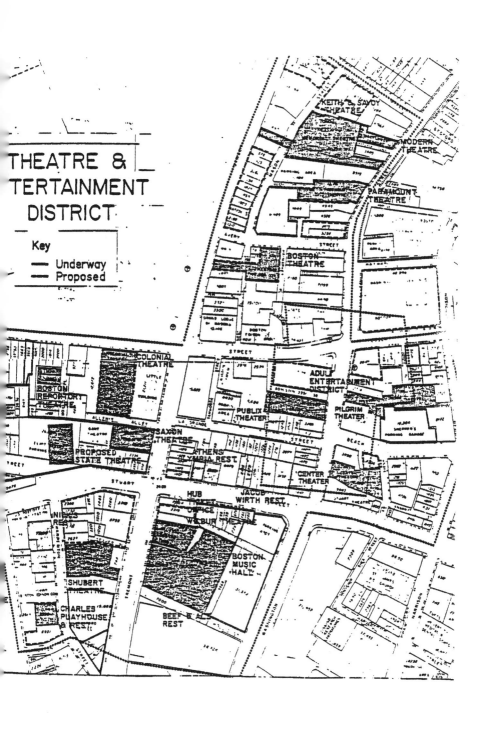

THEATRE &
TERTAINMENT
DISTRICT

Key
—— Underway
—— Proposed

ACKNOWLEDGEMENTS

This report was funded jointly by The Ford Foundation and the Boston Redevelopment Authority to assist in implementation of a comprehensive master plan for the revitalization of Boston's Theatre District.

As members of the study team, Professor Peter Langer, Ph.D, Boston University; Claire Paradiso, M.A., Boston University and Cheryl Gaudreault, M.A., Boston University carried out extensive interviews and assembled data on the sociological implications of the economic transition underway in the Theatre District.

Also, special thanks are extended to the members of the Theatre District Organizing Committee and especially Sister Barbara Scanlon, Chairperson of the Social Services Subcommittee, for the advocacy role played in integrating a social planning concept into the economic and physical planning process.

Finally, we would like to acknowledge the cooperation of over thirty community organizations, service providers and City of Boston agencies in sharing collected data and personal perspectives of issues identified in this report.

CONTENTS

SCOPE OF REPORT

In preparing to undertake this report, it was acknowledged that an attempt to document the social worlds which make up much of the reality and public perception of the Adult Entertainment District would be difficult to structure and almost impossible to disseminate to those who must deal, on a daily basis, with the issues and problems of the "Zone". However, there is clearly a need to separate fact from image as new development in the area begins to exert pressure for dramatic social and economic change.

This report is intended to assist the Boston Redevelopment Authority and City of Boston agencies involved with this change to better comprehend the linkage and implications of the economic rebirth of Boston's Theatre Distrct and the social worlds which have become established in the area.

Clearly this section of the central business district is a unique mixture of urban activity. Legitimate theater, small retail shops, elderly and artists housing share the District with adult entertainment operations, abandoned buildings and vacant lots. Chinatown residents, theater patrons, business-men and tourists pass through the area on sidewalks shared with prostitutes, youth gangs and derelicts. It is an area that has suffered the loss of major department stores and local service outlets but in recent years has been the primary focus of the local performing arts scene.

To many who work and live in the metropolitan area, adult entertainment dominates their perception of the Theatre District. The existence and impact of adult entertainment activities has been identified as the major reason for disinvestment or abandonment of businesses and property. The 1979 theater audience survey carried out by the Mayor's Office of Cultural Affairs and the Boston Redevelopment Authority, and supported by The Ford Foundation, indicated that one of the greatest factors discouraging attendance was the inhospitable environment of the area. The adult bookstores, clubs and movie houses create the vision of the District as decrepit and offensive. The activi-ties, however, are legally controlled and contained within the special zoning boundaries established by the City in 1976 to prevent the spread of these operations to other neighborhoods. It can be argued, however, that it is the threatening street activity that affects most dramatically the physical and perceptive response of Bostonians to the area and this activity, by nature, is fluid in that it can and does easily move from one neighborhood to another.

This then, is the dilemma facing the revitalization of Boston's Theatre District. While the area begins to be influenced by development investment with the accompanying rise in expectations of those who live or have maintained busi-nesses there during the period of economic and social decline, a solution must be found for the continuing existence of the Adult Entertainment District. While housing becomes a more apparent use in the area, what considerations should be made to enhance the environment for residents?

This report then, offers further insights into the dynamics of the Adult Entertainment District and will provide the basis for discussion and public decisions that will influence the area during a period of intense transition and development. It seeks to translate the diverse social worlds that are largely overlooked or misunderstood and relates them to economic development plans

that are taking shape in the minds of planners. It also serves as a presenta
tion of the thoughts, ideas and suggestions of the neighborhoods which have
lived with these social worlds since 1976.

PHYSICAL DEVELOPMENT PATTERN

The existing physical structures of the Adult Entertainment District evolved over a time to produce a diverse collection of small and large buildings of a variety of styles. In general, the area is presently characterized by dilapidated structures, a high vacancy rate in upper stories, small irregular parcels with diverse ownership and numerous public and private alleys which do not function well for either general traffic or servicing.

To date, redevelopment activity has been concentrated to the east of Washington Street, where a series of large, single use, one block buildings have been or are about to be constructed.

Along Washington Street itself, recent pedestrian improvements have re-emphasized the importance of this area as Boston's downtown retail core. As additional retail development is constructed, particularly the Lafayette Place complex, it is planned that these improvements will be extended south to West Street. Tufts-New England Medical Center has begun an expansion of its facilities thus intensifying institutional use along the southern edge of the Adult Entertainment District.

At the same time, retail, restaurant and service activities of the Chinese community are expanding outward from their traditional center on Beach Street. Chinese housing has recently been approved for a location on Essex Street. The area connects the now reviving upper Washington Street theaters (Modern, Savoy/Opera House, Paramount) with the cluster of legitimate houses around the intersection of Stuart and Tremont Street (Metropolitan Center, Wilbur, Shubert, Charles and Colonial).

Clearly, the Adult Entertainment District lies at the intersection of these four development forces and, in fact, five of the remaining fifteen theatre structures within the Theatre District are inside the adult entertainment zoning district. These are the Publix, Pilgrim, Center, Stuart and State Theatres.

The overwhelming characteristic of the Theatre District is its mix of uses and activities, which give a sense of life to the area. While the City certainly wishes to decrease pornography and hostile street activity within the Adult Entertainment District, the finely grained diversity of uses there and throughout the Theatre District should be preserved.

PHYSICAL DEVELOPMENT OBJECTIVES

The Adult Entertainment District straddles Washington Street and its impact on the central business district influences the Boston Common and the Public Garden, three of the most imageable and unique features of the City. The prominence of this area is a primary reason why it has become an area of intense development interest. However, the locale also demands a need for sensitive design and placement of new construction and renovation to avoid negative impacts.

Avoidance of shadows on the Common is an overriding consideration. The City has established a height restriction of 155 feet for new structures within 100 feet of the Common. The long public debate over the Park Plaza Urban Renewal Project has established a consensus that structures in the vicinity of the Common and Public Garden should be limited to 30 stories. This approximates the average height of existing towers in the area. Therefore, the placement of the highest new structure should be the furthest from this area.

Along Washington Street, pedestrian improvements have been made or are being planned to re-emphasize this area of Boston's retail core. As a transition zone between the retail core, the Theatre District and Chinatown, sensitive planning decisions will be made to support and reinforce the diverse economic activity on Wasington Street and to accommodate the increasing residential character of side streets including West, Essex and Beach Streets. Therefore new development should be located in this area with a sense of providing a visual terminus to the downtown retail core and the beginning of the Theatre District. Adjacent to Washington Street, the traditional 6-8 story cornice line should be respected by setting back any new towers. In general, sensitivity to the present scale and character of surrounding buildings will enhance the quality and acceptability of proposed projects.

ACCESS

The area is well served by public transportation. The Orange Line Essex Station can be entered from either side of Washington Street and the Green Line Boylston Station is located in the Common at Tremont Street. In addition an abandoned exit for the Orange Line Essex Station is located on LaGrange Street, the most notorious street in the Adult Entertainment District, while a new $65 million South Cove Orange Line Station is being constructed adjacent to Washington Street just to the south of Stuart/Kneeland Streets.

As mentioned earlier, a primary pedestrian access route to the Theatre District will be from the north via Washington Street/Downtown Crossing. As additional retail development occurs, plans call for these improvements to be extended southward. A logical terminus for these pedestrian improvements would be the Liberty Square area, which could be linked to provide a transition to Chinatown. Vehicular circulation may continue on Avery, West and Lower Washington Streets to maintain a westerly flow to Tremont Street, provide access to Lafayette Place and serve to facilitate passenger delivery to theatres.

Other vehicle and pedestrian improvements are connected with the Park Plaza Urban Renewal Project where Stuart Street, Boylston Street, Tremont Street and Charles Street will receive basic roadway construction including street lighting, signing, traffic signals and landscaping.

Warrenton Place, Warrenton Street and the Shubert parking lot will become pedestrian ways connected through the State Transportation Building to Boylston Street.

HOUSING

In recent years, the City and private developers have shown increasing interest in developing housing in the Theatre District. Thus far, primarily elderly housing has been constructed at 80 Mason Street, the R.H. Stearn's Building and the soon to begin renovation of the former Normandy Hotel. Housing is a desirable use because it provides a local resident market for retail and entertainment operations.

In general, most new housing development will continue to be aimed at one of two markets; subsidized units for the elderly and Chinese and luxury accommodations, particularly along the Common where the spectacular views and convenient proximity to shopping, services and employment sites will be strong motivation for site selection.

RETAIL

The much hoped for renaissance of Washington Street is now underway, including the completion of the first phase of Downtown Crossing, the construction of Lafayette Place and the possible future development of a third major department store on the southerly parcel of Lafayette Place.

Additional retail activity will occupy ground level space in the new State Transportation Building on Stuart Street. This may be viewed as part of a gradual eastward expansion of the Boylston Street retail spine.

At the same time, retail, restaurant and service activities of the Chinese community are expanding westward from the neighborhood core area of Beach Street and Harrison Avenue.

The City is encouraging ground floor commercial/retail uses in new developments along Washington Street and is in the process of establishing a Commercial Area Revitalization District (C.A.R.D.) designation for the entire Theatre District/Chinatown core area.

Although new retail growth is extremely desirable, it carries with it some sensitive issues with regard to scale of new construction and economic impact. With the first issue, modern retailing practices encourage large floor areas with as few levels as possible and controlled pedestrian access to the facility to create a captive market situation where potential customers can find every need within the confines of the structure. This has, and will continue to result in predominantly three-story buildings to the east of Washington Street, which is somewhat incompatible with the 6-8 story structures on the west side of the street, and with limited contribution to passive pedestrian activity on the street itself. Additionally, the reality of a continued growth in the number and variety of large chain store operations that will occupy space in these new retail centers will force a reappraisal of marketing conditions on existing, small businesses which line Washington Street today.

With the City's objective of continuing ground floor retail uses and extension of the Downtown Crossing concept, design decisions will have to be made to relate new large scale commercial development to the commercial street life of the area. The local neighborhood associations and City should provide technical assistance to existing small retailers to enhance the possibilities for their continued viability in a changing market.

Finally, the Adult Entertainment District itself lies at the intersection of these retail/commercial development forces. Development proposals for this area can help to resolve these forces by providing secondary retail outlets competitive space in renovated buildings and by serving to define and provide the final linking of Washington Street, Boylston Street and Chinatown commercial areas. Pedestrian movement along these three retail areas will be encouraged by the dissipation of perceived hostile street actions and the increased utilization of vacant building space by legitimate commercial activity.

ENTERTAINMENT

Performing arts and entertainment are the primary economic activities which
give the area an identification. The Publix, Pilgrim, Center and Paramount
theatre buildings offer the potential specialized space to accommodate Boston':
burgeoning performing arts industry. Each of these theatres, which present
are either vacant, used for pornographic presentations or serve the neighbor
hood entertainment needs of Chinatown, could be restored to house a variety
of national or local theatre groups seeking facilities within the Theatre Distri

Should these four theatres begin to attract the growing audience for live
perfomances in theatre, dance or music, a strong unifying force will be
established to connect the reviving upper Washington Street theatres (Modern
Opera House) with the cluster of legitimate commercial theatre around the
intersection of Stuart and Tremont Streets (Wilbur, Metropolitan Center,
Shubert, Colonial and Charles Playhouse).

Pedestrian amenities are being planned at locations which will encourage use
by legitimate theatre-goers as well as provide for general public safety.

New development projects being proposed for the study area, while composed
mainly of housing and retail use, should be encouraged to provide for the
rehabilitation of these theatre structures or include programmatic elements
which will strengthen the unique cultural, tourist and residential mix which i:
beginning to emerge as the future character of lower Washington and Stuart
Streets.

SOCIAL PLANNING

As indicated, important changes are slated for Boston's Theatre District in regard to economic development and housing. In order to proceed with these developments in a way which is most beneficial to the City as a whole, it is important to recognize how this area of the City presently operates as a social entity, and what social or human consequences might result from the physical transition. This section of the report reflects the concerns of the Social Planning Task Force of the Theatre District Organizing Committee of the Boston Redevelopment Authority.

Interviews were conducted with representatives of groups and organizations associated with the Theatre District, and who are critically related to the area as a whole. These groups fall into the following types:

    (1) Civic and neighborhood associations.
    (2) Social service providers.
    (3) Government agencies.
    (4) Other individuals knowledgeable about the area.

The following is a listing of the interviewed parties:

Civic and Neighborhood Associations

Chinese American Civic Association (CACA)
Bay Village Neighborhood Association (BVNA)
Park Plaza Civic Advisory Council
Stuart Street Neighborhood Association (SSNA)
Back Bay Association
Downtown Crossing Association
Washington & Tremont Neighborhood Association (WTNA)
80 Mason Street House Council
Quincy School Community Council
Chinese Economic Development Council (CEDC)
Chinese Consolidated Benevolent Association (CCBA)

Social Service Providers

Action for Boston Community Development (ABCD)
Project Place Runaway House
The Salvation Army
Tufts-New England Medical Center (T-NEMC)
The Bridge, Inc.
Many Mansions
The Paulist Center
Pine Street Inn
Traveler's Aid
South Cove YMCA
Youth Essential Services, Inc. (YES)
Homophile Community Health Center
South Cove Community Health Center
Greater South Cove Golden Age Center
Rosie's Place
Gay Hot Line

Government Agencies

Boston Redevelopment Authority (BRA)
Office of Cultural Affairs
Office of Public Safety
Boston Police Department
Youth Activities Commission
Office of Program Development
Office of Human Rights
Boston Elderly Commission
Boston-Chinatown Little City Hall
Boston Licensing Division
Boston Licensing Board
Boston Juvenile Court
Massachusetts Blue Ribbon Common on Deinstitutionalization

Others

The Artists' Foundation
State Street Development Corporation
Tremont-on-the-Common
Wilbur Theatre
Metropolitan Center
Church of All Nations
Individual Restaurateurs
Individual Theatre and Club Proprietors
Individual Merchants
Independent Street Workers

In total, ninety-five (95) individuals were interviewed at length and information was received from others in less formal settings.

The information that follows is based on these interviews and observations of the area. This report is, thus, an analysis of what the most knowledgeable individuals report about the Adult Entertainment District and their opinions about what they report. The analysis concentrates on presenting the social situation of the area as it really is, but goes beyond a mere reporting of what informants reported to indicate patterns of conflict and consensus, assumptions, and potential areas of concern.

The social reality of the Adult Entertainment District, Theatre District and the broader area of which they are a part is addressed in the following section.

DOWNTOWN NEIGHBORHOOD

There are as many impressions of the Theatre District area as there are interest groups in the City. Interviews have been consistent in only one way -- everyone agrees that this is a special section of the City of Boston. This uniqueness may be lauded or it may be vilified, but it is agreed that things happen here that happen nowhere else in the City. What are the characteristics which make this section of the City seem unusual to people?

The dominant characteristic of the District is its _diversity_, both in terms of land use and in the _people_ who populate the area.

The diversity of land use in the area is visible and clear. There is the large institutional presence of Tufts-New England Medical Center and its expanding physical plant. There are the legitimate theatres which many believe anchor the District, but which are distributed in several different sites so that their total impact is much less than the sum of their parts. There is the strong impact of the Adult Entertainment District which through its concentration and its gaudiness projects throughout the area. There is Chinatown with its commercial activity and growing residential population. There are the businesses north of Boylston Street. There are the scattered offices of social service and non-profit agencies. There are the residential buildings of Tremont-on-the-Common, the Hotel Touraine, 80 Mason Street, and other scattered units often above ground floor commercial activity. There is the tightly knit residential neighborhood of Bay Village adjacent to some of the legitimate theatres. There are schools and churches. There is light manufacturing in loft spaces. And there are empty parcels and parking lots seemingly poised to see which way the area moves.

It is an area with the commercial, office, cultural, and institutional land uses characteristic of a _downtown_ along with the growing residential components of a _neighborhood_. The distinctive aspect of the area is one of becoming a _downtown neighborhood_.

The essential ingredient of a downtown neighborhood is not the range and diversity of land use in the area since all neighborhoods have some such diversity, but rather the _diversity of people_ who make use of this land. Downtowns attract people from throughout the metropolis, whereas neighborhoods characteristically are more enclosed and oriented to the needs of their particular residential population. The area of the Theatre District, however, as a downtown neighborhood, must accommodate both residents and non-residents, including out-of-towners who are more and more attracted to Boston. The diversity of people in the area can be set forth in the following three types:

1.   Residents

Residents of the Theatre District area include the professional couples of Tremont-on-the-Common and Bay Village, the elderly of 80 Mason Street, the middle class and working people of Chinatown and the Hotel Touraine, the cooks, bartenders and waiters of the clubs and restaurants in the area, new immigrants squeezing into the already overcrowded spaces in Chinatown, and the medical students housed by Tufts-New England Medical Center.

2. Regulars

Regulars are identified as people who do not live in the area but who regularly use the District for work or leisure and live in the Boston metropolitan area. This category includes people who are thought of as very beneficial to the area as well as people who are regarded as problems for the area. In the first group there are the people who own businesses or work in the area, the shoppers, restaurant users, and theatre-goers. In the second group there are homeless men and women, prostitutes, muggers and others who prey upon the people passing through the area.

3. Transients

Transients are people from out of town who pass through the area. They are also divided into two groups. Tourists and conventioneers patronize legitimate theatres, the Adult Entertainment District, restaurants, and shops. There are also the transients who are homeless or drifting, young people seeking refuge on the Boston Common, and adults and families disoriented or in need of aid.

No other section of Boston has such a combination of diverse residents, regulars and transients. This report will be returning to these types as it sketches out the differing needs, resources and services which these different groups of people require.

Diverse in land use and in population, the Theatre District area is regarded by some as in desperate need of change and revitalization, and by others as a unique area which should be upgraded and not destroyed. Different views of the diversity of the area are illustrated by the following remarks.

As one social service agency administrator puts it:

> "We are located here because we have clients coming in from all over the City. This location is critical to us because it is neutral turf. People of all ethnicities and races can come here. It is safe and neutral, along with being accessible and centrally located. One would be hard pressed to find another place from which one could serve the entire City."

The point she makes about what she calls the "neutrality" of the area is critical to our assessment of the area. Boston is a city of neighborhoods from which members of differing races and ethnic groups are often excluded or themselves avoid in order not to endanger themselves. Because most of Boston's neighborhoods are so tightly controlled by particular social groups, downtown areas which are open to people of different races are of particular importance.

However, many people feel the diversity of the area harbors elements destructive to the area. As one local businessman puts it: "Anything would be better than what we have now."

Most businessmen feel that the area is in drastic need of changes that will bring more residents and more shoppers into the area. They feel that the

people who pass through the area without patronizing their businesses are
threats to their legitimate patrons and create a negative image for the whole
area.

The Theatre District then is an area that is diverse, populated by many
different types of people, but which is regarded as in need of drastic change
by the people who have financial interests in the area. This change revolves
around their concern with the perceptions of safety and crime and the delete-
rious effect that has on their businesses. Is it possible to improve the
economic climate of the area and keep the openness, accessibility and diversity
of a downtown neighborhood? A critical element of an affirmative answer to
this question lies in the public perception of the causes of crime and the
factors of public safety in the area.

A Community View of Public Safety

In discussing safety in the area one must deal with the perception of safety
as one moves from the Common through the side streets connecting Tremont
and Washington Streets, from upper Washington to lower Washington Street,
from the Combat Zone to Chinatown, Tufts-New England Medical Center,
South Cove, Bay Village, and the Theatre District. One must also view
safety through the eyes of those who live, work or pass through the downtown
area, and one must further understand how people's perception of safety is
connected with the time of day and night, their age, and their "street sense".

It was found in interviews with community residents and representatives that
the actual crime rate and security of the area is much less important than the
poor image people have of it. This is not to say that the safety concerns of
people are irrelevant and unimportant, but rather that people's fears are
products of the downtown environment. Boston's downtown environment has
yet to fully evolve into a neighborhood environment with the physical amenities
and social activities which would make the area more secure for its residents.
Yet, this area, as part of the downtown core, serves other purposes while
still maintaining its essential character as a downtown -- a cosmopolitan,
metropolitan and community center for business, government and the arts.

Daytime: Nine to Five Business Hours

During the business day, when the streets are crowded with pedestrians and
cars, perceptions of safety in the area are similar to those of the rest of the
downtown. The types of crime associated with daytime activities are generally
non-violent -- store thefts or shoplifting, purse snatching, pickpocketing,
and breaking and entering. Other factors affecting the daytime perception of
the area are related to image problems -- the negative image of the Combat
Zone, the avoidance of dirty streets and alleyways, the aversion to homeless
men and women.

Businesses are clearly concerned with people's perceptions of the area, robbery
and shoplifting. One group of businessmen and women referred to the Combat
Zone as a "sanctuary for predators", stating:

> "The Zone is a hideout for every unpleasant and illegal activity
> that goes on around here. Shoplifters will retreat into the
> Zone. They don't hide in Government Center; they go there.
> The area is a place where they hide."

Another businessperson, thinking of increased pedestrian activity and hence more potential customers, talked of "non-threatening" appearances and uses along the pedestrian path from Quincy Market to the Theatre District:

> "If Boston develops the way we hope it will, with a continuation of the return to the City movement, there is a natural walking path from Quincy Market down Washington Street and to the Theatre District. To have such a path you have to have non-threatening appearances and non-threatening uses of the area."

The smaller businesses on lower Washington Street are well aware of images of the area and would like to see the Downtown Crossing, which has been a boon to upper Washington Street, extended at least to Boylston Street. Along with their desire to be part of the public improvement program, the lower Washington Street businesses desire an increased police presence, especially since they border on the Combat Zone.

> "You want to know what kind of a bad image the lower Washington Street legitimate businesses have. Over Washington's Birthday, I handed out over 3,500 leaflets describing all the stores in this area and hardly anyone looked at the pamphlet and those that did said they wouldn't shop there because they thought it was part of the Combat Zone. There was a quarter of a million people in the Downtown Crossing that day, and only a few thousand on my end of the block."

Thus, the lower Washington Street businesses feel that they not only have to deal with competition from the larger department stores, and pilferage, but also feel that they are being neglected and may be forced out of business unless the City helps them deal with the threat of the Combat Zone.

Although the daylight hours appear to be the safest for shoppers and resident it is evident that this is due to the density of people in the area and the presence of police at the Downtown Crossing. Speaking of the decline in purse snatching after the completion of the Downtown Crossing project, one member of the Washington-Tremont Neighborhood Association asked if police would be stationed on "this end of Washington Street" (lower Washington Street) after Lafayette Place is built. Indicating a resident's perception of the relation of crime to a police presence is the following comment made at the same neighborhood meeting:

> "People don't commit crimes where police are located. There are 600,000 people in this City and they all want policemen. And these kids aren't stupid; they know there's a shift at 4:00 p.m. and that all the police are at the stationhouse changing shifts then. So that's when they hit and run."

At another meeting of this group in March, an elderly resident of 80 Mason Street said:

> "Footpatrols... we need more of them, and more than that. We saw someone attacked at 3:00 p.m. We know, we see what goes on out there... that was about four weeks ago."

Many of the residents of 80 Mason Street, who are either handicapped or
elderly, feel that they are prime candidates for muggers and purse snatchers
and would like to see an armed security guard for their building. Such a
guard could leave the building premises to protect and escort them to their
cars or to Tremont or Washington Streets.

Many of the issues concerning safety for Chinese residents during the day
time are similar to those of other residents of the area. When we asked those
knowledgeable about Chinatown whether the Chinese population was victimized
by the Combat Zone which borders Chinatown proper, we received comments
similar to the following:

"Around the Zone the derelicts are more of a nuisance. They
hang around and pass out in front of the Chinese American
Civic Association offices, which discourages people from approach-
ing for services."

Some of the crime in Chinatown has been attributed to the prostitutes who
mug people and vandalize homes. According to one respondent, "The pimps
create many of the problems in Chinatown by forcing their prostitutes to rob
people when business is off." According to another informant:

"The prostitutes aren't the ones who are responsible for a lot
of crime, and they, in fact, are victims of crimes, since they're
robbed and beaten by johns, and even robbed by the police.
A lot of the crime that goes on is done by 'mug boys' and
'mug girls' who are teenagers who pose as prostitutes to rob
johns. They pick their pockets."

Although some crime is linked to prostitution in one form or another, many
Chinese will admit that crime is also an internal community problem related to
Chinese youth gangs. While it is unclear what the actual structure of the
gangs are and how teenagers become involved in them, they appear to emanate
from outside Boston and have led to the Chinese community taking steps to
control them. According to one source, "The gangs are made up of kids from
Hong Kong, who come to Boston directly from Hong Kong or from New York
or San Fransisco... These kids have come here to get rich and they do it by
illegitimate means. Their objective is to take over--to control drugs, prostitution, the numbers, but it hasn't worked in Boston because we're small enough
to control them." In terms of the numbers and strengths of the gangs, one
person knowledgeable about the Chinese community said that "Boston is three
hundreds times better than New York or San Francisco." He added, "One of
the problems with these gangs is that, when very organized, victims are wont
to report crimes such as robbery. Tai Tung Village had been infiltrated by a
New York gang, but the residents there have set up their own security and
the problem has dissipated." Yet, according to another informant, the gangs
are still a serious problem:

"The youth gangs which Chinese kids are involved with are
part of bigger gangs in New York, which are similar and
connected to those in San Fransisco. They are mainly into
extortion, drugs, and kidnapping. Kidnapping hasn't been
big in Boston yet, though it's prevalent among Chinese gangs
in New York and will most likely increase here as the groups

- 13 -

become more established and gain enough adherents. Both
boys and girls, between the ages of thirteen and twenty, are
involved in these gangs. There are sex related role distinctions within the gangs: the boys get involved in extortion
and kidnapping and drugs, while the girls are pushed into
prostitution."

Nighttime: The Early Evening and Late Night

As night falls and the downtown empties of people, some businesses shut
down, the stores close, and the Combat Zone, Theatre District and the restaurants and bars come to life, the image of the area changes drastically. For
women and the elderly especially, the entire area becomes a zone of potential
muggers and rapists. For women, there is added the constant confrontation
with men treating them as prostitutes and propositioning them. As one woman
related a common incident: "Women are hassled all the time. I was waiting
for the bus near Boylston and I was bundled up from head to toe with a
scarf wrapped around my face because it was cold and windy, and this man
approached me, and this was around 5:30 or 6:00, and propositioned me."
Women who are theatre goers are also afraid to park in the garages in the
Theatre District, claiming that they are dark and unpatrolled. Said one
woman:

"The parking garages are very unsafe and I'd rather park on
the street in front of a fire hydrant than park in a garage. I
think this is an important issue for the increasing numbers of
women attending the theatre."

As the evening approaches, residents, especially the elderly residents, desire
better street lighting and a neighborhood foot patrol. As a member of the
Washington-Tremont Neighborhood Association voiced at a meeting, "So many
of us older people simply do not go out after dark." The residents at 80 Masc
Street also fear that what they perceive as inadequate building security will
be cut back rather than increased.

"The day security Monday through Friday from 8:00 to 4:00
will not be provided any longer. Blackstone Elderly Apartments
on the site of the Blackstone School built by State Street
(State Street Developers is also the one which built 80 Mason
Street) started with full security and now has none. They
don't have the Zone there, it is safer; there are a lot of
people coming and going from Mass. General Hospital and
Holiday Inn."

"Security through State Street is lax. It's ineffective and
superficial. At Mason Street the guard stays in his office.
He should look on the parking lot at least once an hour. He
just sits in the lobby and watches the monitor."

It is clearly evident that whether they attribute crime and violence directly or
indirectly to the Combat Zone or to the breakdown of social institutions, such
as the family, neighborhood groups are affected by their image of the safety
of the area. One life-long resident of Chinatown discussed how things have
changed since he was growing up in the 1940's and 1950's:

"When I was a kid in what you might call the golden age of
the 40's and 50's, people in Chinatown would sit on their
stoops, and in the evening they would go up Washington
Street and window shop. Now it's unsafe after dark."

Bay Village copes with the problem through its citizen volunteer patrol. As
one Bay Village Neighborhood Association (BVNA) member explained to us:

"Our main concern is not so much prostitution as it is the
violence that goes along with it, along with the traffic and the
trash. BVNA is concerned because as Park Square changes,
some of their problems may come over here."

Another BVNA member interjected this comment:

"Prostitution is not a victimless crime: punks rob the prostitutes,
all women become solicited on the street, and people defecate
and urinate in the street."

Of concern to others is the safety of the Theatre District itself: "Little
banners on the light poles saying this is a theatre district are nice, but
people have to walk from Park Street without being maimed." Others have
stressed not only that they feel that the Boston Common Garage, where some
theatre goers park, is unsafe, but that they avoid walking through the
Common itself to get to the theatres, since it is deserted at night and not
well lit.

In addition to safety there are other explanations for low theatre attendance:

"There are two major problems for the Theatre District.
First, ticket prices, which is probably the most important
factor in keeping people away because they're too high.
Second is the safety issue which is tied to the Combat Zone
and the fear of the area. This is a physical and policing
problem. There is no more crime in this area than in the
suburbs. What is needed are physical plans that will encourage
around the clock activity. The City is designing pedestrian
malls which are well lit, which will connect the Boylston "T"
stop and the two parking garages at Tufts and the Howard
Johnson's with the major theatres."

This report has discussed safety from the point of view of the community. It
will now turn to a discussion of crime and safety as seen by the police who
work in the area.

Police View of Area

Similar to resident's perceptions of the area, police officers view various
problems occurring at different times of the day. During the daylight hours,
police officers feel that the area is "just like any other part of downtown",
and is not particularly problemmatic. During the evening hours between six

and midnight, street traffic in the area is such that there are usually no problems for people who are going about their business and not looking for any "action". One officer who has worked in the area for over ten years says:

> "There are not many problems with theatre-goers being mugged. When the theatres are going there are lots of people on the street, so there aren't any problems, and that holds true even if people go out for drinks or dinner afterwards. The problems begin after midnight when the people from the clubs are starting to do a lot of drinking and the clubs are starting to close."

Problems with mugging and assaults arise between midnight and 3 a.m. This is also the time when there are many cars cruising, searching for prostitutes:

> "You wouldn't believe the cruising that goes on -- at 3 a.m. there is so much traffic you need to have a traffic detail directing it!"

Although the police do everything they can to protect the people from assaults and muggings, they usually feel that the people who are out on the streets at this time of night are "asking for trouble".

Since the police do not have the resources to cover the area all the time in the way many residents and businesses wish they would, they find themselves working in response to citizen complaints:

> "It's frustrating dealing with prostitution. It's a revolving door. They get a $50 fine, the courts do nothing and they are back on the street. But in spite of that frustration we have to do it when it gets heavy and out of control -- when we get complaints from every corner from theatre-goers to restaurant owners. We try to keep up on it."

Most people in the area feel that the police do a good job in keeping up on the problem. One of the owners who is greatly concerned about prostitution in the area has this to say:

> "For me, the time when police surveillance is most important is during the theatre times and for an hour or so afterwards -- up until midnight. For my friends and customers the prostitution is an embarrassment and a harrassment. The situation was worse a few years back and the police have responded to pressure to clean it up. The police have done a hell of a job. But as long as the Zone is there the police can't do much more than what they are doing."

While most people concur with the view that the police are doing a good job dealing with a difficult situation, some are unhappy with the police presence in the area. One resident says:

> "The police are not really receptive to our needs. Our problem is the prostitutes and the people who come to prey on them

and their customers, and the police don't regard prostitution
as one of their priorities. They don't really harrass the
prostitutes."

It is indeed true that the police department's present budgetary and manpower
restrictions prevent them from providing ideal service to the area, but it is
also true that the police respond to legitimate demands of residents. However,
many police officers do not regard the area as having much of a residential
population; and they definitely do not regard it as a "neighborhood". To the
·police this is a "downtown" and they treat it as such. But, to them, it is a
special part of the downtown because it has the Combat Zone in it and the
Zone creates problems for everyone concerned.

COMBAT ZONE

Everyone has an opinion about the Adult Entertainment District -- the "Combat
Zone" -- and its influence on the surrounding area. In many ways the
central concern of the developers and officials involved in the revitalization of
the Theatre District lies in how the Combat Zone affects the area and how to
deal with these effects. The views of the Combat Zone divide into two camps. .
One views the Zone as the cause of all problems and something which must be
eliminated. The second sees the Zone as just one part of the area and something with which they can learn to live. In an elaboration of these views,
the following comments bring forth the key aspects of the Zone and its place
in the area as a whole.

The Zone as the Root of All Problems - A Perspective

"The Zone? The City would be better off without it -- the
area is depressed because of it. Get rid of it. Level it. Get
rid of the (sleazy) joints. Get rid of the perverts and de-
generates who go there. Legitimate people are not interested
in this trash. Get that cancer out of there."

"The Zone? Move it to Worcester! Get rid of the thing!
Whose bright idea was it anyway? It's nothing but a big
expense and a big headache. Prostitutes bounce from one
corner to another. You can't contain it. It's a cesspool."

These comments by police officers represent one strong opinion toward the
Zone.

The different police officers and officials interviewed are united in their
condemnation of the officially created Adult Entertainment District:

"When they put in the Zone they created what someone has
called 'an illusion of license' -- telling people they are free to
do what they want there. People go to the porno places and
then go one step further and get involved with the street girls
and then the trouble begins."

The police feel that the problems of the Zone makes them put resources there
which could be used in other areas of downtown Boston. They feel they are
putting too many police resources into the area already.

- 17 -

For many businessmen in the area the Zone is the problem which is keeping the area from being more financially successful. At the meeting of a local business association feelings about the Zone were very clearly expressed by one candidate for office in the association:

> "As a businessman, I want this area to be as profitable as
> possible. I want it also to be as comfortable and secure as
> possible. I want to work in an area people do not say is 'on
> the edge of the Combat Zone'."

Business leaders regard the Zone as inhibiting the area, because as one of them says, "the City has to take a major role in development because without its initiative private enterprise doesn't want to touch the area because of the Combat Zone."

Not only is private investment supposedly deterred because of the presence of the Zone, but certain federal and foundation monies are said to be held up because these sources want to see something done about the Zone first.

It is not just businessmen who are concerned about the Combat Zone. Many social service workers are concerned with the effect the Zone has on young people who pass through the area and to the residents who must live near it. A person who works primarily with teenagers says:

> "They should bring in a lot of bulldozers, dynamite the place
> and level the whole Zone. Kids see the fancy cars, the big
> money and the flashy window dressing that goes with the
> Zone. The problem is, how do you get kids out of this? What
> do we have to offer them in exchange? The authorities don't
> care about these kids. They feel that these kids are maggots
> anyhow. They're from the other side of town, from the projects,
> their parents are messed up. So the cops won't do much. I'd
> like to see greater public awareness of the problem. I'd like
> to see public outrage over some of these things that go on in
> the Combat Zone. I'd like to see more law enforcement and a
> crackdown especially on the 'kiddie hawks' and the kiddie
> pornographic rings that kids get sucked into."

The view of most social service people is that the adults who come to the area are there knowing what they are doing and if they are victimized they are at least somewhat to blame for not knowing how to handle themselves. This is not the case for many of the kids in the area:

> "We have to police this area better. If adults want to do
> something -- that's OK. Just don't take advantage of the
> kids! We have to do something to protect the kids who are
> downtown everyday truant from the Boston schools. These
> kids get taken in by con-men and 'pepsi-cola pimps'. And
> then there are the people like this theatre agent who gets
> phony ID's for minors and puts them into the strip joints. We
> go in cycles of reaction to the Zone, when we should be constantly
> enforcing the laws."

For some of the young people of Chinatown the dangers of the Combat Zone are seen as more pervasive and as much psychological in nature as physical. A social worker from Chinatown states:

"Many of the teenagers from the mainland (China) in particular cannot handle the culture shock of the Zone. Many of them will walk all around the periphery of the Zone, out of their way, since they're actually afraid of the pictures of the naked girls. Many of them hadn't even seen a blond female before coming here. Remember that traditional Chinese culture doesn't encourage physical touching; these cultural extremes clash. This situation leads to a proliferation of mental health problems. Some kids, on the other hand, go see X-rated movies and hang around the Zone" (without any negative effects).

Another social agency administrator stresses the nighttime impact of the Combat Zone on Chinatown:

"Anyone who says that the Combat Zone does not create a lot of problems for Chinatown residents doesn't live here. Sure, the Combat Zone isn't much of a problem in the daytime; it's at night when it becomes a problem, especially around two and three o'clock in the morning. Prostitutes use our doorways, apartments get ripped off, dope dealing goes on, hookers and pimps are all over the place, and cars are being stolen.

My backyard was swept clean the other day, but I could take you back there now and you'd find four or five prophylactics on the ground. I close the gates, but the prostitutes get in anyway.

We're used to the congestion and traffic, the car horns blow-ing at night. This isn't the real concern, the real concern is with safety and decency. We don't like prostitution on our front steps or in our backyards."

Depression of land values, harrassment of residents, seduction of young people -- all of these features are attributed to the Combat Zone. In the view of these people the Zone must be eliminated if anything good is going to happen to this area of the City.

<u>The Zone is Limited in its Impact</u>

For an equal number of people the Zone is merely one part of the entire area, and while it has its unpleasant aspects it is neither an unmitigated disaster nor the cause of all the problems in the Theatre District.

The limited nature of the Combat Zone is expressed by the following small businessman located south of Stuart Street:

"Crime is kept under control here by the merchants who know who the crooks are. You never see any pimps or prostitutes around here, do you? That's because they know I won't let them hang around here. The Combat Zone has no influence on this block. I have no control over the Combat Zone. I'm not a merchant there. This is the Theatre District, and it has its own world."

In the view of this person, who calls himself the "policeman of Tremont Street the Zone is indeed a rotten place, but a place whose boundaries are limited and which does not have much effect on people who do not voluntarily ventur into the area during the evenings. For him the area is not exclusively define by the Combat Zone, but is, rather, a combination of smaller worlds with thei own lives and their own means of controlling their streets. A person who worked as a street-worker in the area for several years expresses a similar point of view:

"The extent of crimes against the Chinese coming out of the Zone is exaggerated. The Zone doesn't want to bring down the Chinese community on them. The Zone polices itself."

And in the eyes of a City official who has watched the Zone grow and change

"Everyone in the Zone knows what they are doing. Very few people are there innocently. Damn few kids are victimized by the Zone because the clubs are very careful not to let them in, or they'd be closed."

Even the police who are the most adamant spokes-people for the evils of the Zone see it as relatively limited in its impact in terms of personal safety and crime. When asked how the activity on the Boston Common relates to the activity in the Zone, one officer responded:

"There is no connection between the Zone and the Common. It's a completely different ball of wax with its own activities and its own people. Chinatown? What about it? Victimized by the activity from the Zone? That's a silly question. The Chinese are not victimized by the Zone. Elderly Chinese are victimized by their own people -- other Chinese -- not by street people from the Zone. The so-called leaders of China-town are always ripping off their own people."

About the connection between Chinatown and the Zone, a well-informed social service worker from Chinatown stated, rather apologetically, when asked about reported muggings of elderly Chinese in the Combat Zone:

"I haven't heard of any muggings, and I'm sure I would be aware of it. I know that some Chinese go to the movies in the Combat Zone, but actually, and I hate to admit this, the Combat Zone seems relatively safe. It's dirty, immoral, and more of a nuisance and embarrassment than anything else."

And some representatives of Bay Village have a similar view of the limited impact of the Zone on their neighborhood:

"The Zone doesn't really impact on us. It affects us when the police crack down on the hookers there, and they temporarily move over to us. The Zone has been in an area that has not been residential, so that was a good place for those types of activities. In a way, I'd like to have it flourish there, because in that parochial sense it doesn't hurt us now."

These different views of the Zone suggest the following distinctions: The first is the distinction among the different sub-areas of the study area with a mapping of the effective boundaries of these different sub-areas. The second is to distinguish between the activity within the businesses of the Adult Entertainment District and the activity on the streets of the entire area. And the third distinction is the importance of the image of the Zone as opposed to the actual activity in the Zone.

The Effective Boundaries of the Combat Zone

Interviews and observations suggest that the "Combat Zone" as a social reality is broader than the boundaries of the officially designated "Adult Entertainment District", but it is not so broad as to dominate the entire area we include in this study. The "effective boundaries" of the Zone are those boundaries which people familiar with the area regard as "really" being a part of the Zone. The following map outlines these effective boundaries and contrasts the Zone with the other sub-areas of the project area.

The Combat Zone is effectively bounded on the south by Stuart Street. This is the sharpest and most distinctive boundary, especially at the corner of Stuart and Washington Streets where the Adult Entertainment District ends officially but also where the Tufts medical buildings contrast sharply with the activity on the other side of Stuart Street.

To the east, many people feel that once they have turned down Beach Street, especially after they have rounded the bend in Beach, they have left the Zone and they are now in Chinatown. There is a point of friction and overlap here, however, because in the evening when the Adult Entertainment District's clubs close, some of the prostitution and street activity moves down Beach to Harrison Avenue. Beach thus provides a conduit for encroachment of the Zone into Chinatown, but this conduit is effectively closed during the day due to the bustling activity on Harrison Avenue in the heart of Chinatown.

The extension of the Zone to the north varies during different times of the day. The boundary at the Boylston-Essex intersection is fairly firm during the day with the office workers and other activity near the 600 Washington Street building acting as a screen between the Zone and another pocket of activity centered around the Amusement Center located at 545 Washington Street. The Amusement Center is regarded as not in the Zone but it is a problem for many people in the area and, along with the closed Paramount Theatre, projects a frightening image to many people.

The western boundary and extension of the Zone is the most problemmatic in terms of its effect on the Theatre District. LaGrange Street, which is universally regarded as the most dangerous and most troublesome street in the area, serves as a passageway for activity from Washington Street to funnel down to Tremont Street. The intersection of LaGrange and Tremont becomes a prime location for prostitution due to this influence of LaGrange Street. This problemmatic intersection is especially visible because it stands right in the pathway of people moving from the Boylston "T" stop, the Common, and the businesses along and above Boylston Street to the central core of the Theatre District located south of Stuart Street.

Basically, the Zone extends east and west beyond the official limits of the Adult Entertainment District. Its southern expansion is stopped by Tufts, and its northern extension by the commercial and office traffic on Washington Street. Although its eastern expansion intrudes on Chinatown it does not critically change the shape or activity of Chinatown. Its western expansion, however, critically affects the Theatre District, because, and this point is critical, the Theatre District itself is divided into several sections and does not have a unifying core. It is this fragmentation of the Theatre District which permits the activity of the Zone to so critically impact on the Theatre District at Tremont Street.

Adult Entertainment District Businesses vs. Combat Zone Street Activity

The most critical distinction we must make in regards to the area known as the "Combat Zone" is the difference between the clubs, adult bookstores and peep shows which are licensed within the Adult Entertainment District and the activities of the people who populate the streets. For many people the busine there are problems because they are assumed to create criminal street activity In order to understand this connection we must first differentiate the two entities. We use the term "Combat Zone" to refer to the social behavior occurring in the area. This behavior is distinct from the businesses licensed within the official Adult Entertainment District.

The connection between the Adult Entertainment District businesses and the street crime and problems in the area is regarded as direct and causal by many people in the area. In the words of a police official quoted earlier, "People go to the porno places and then go one step further and get involved with the street girls and then the trouble begins." This officer continues:

> "It's the clients of the clubs that attract the street pimps.
> The action is on the streets and in the cars. Most of the
> action is very quick -- a guy picking up a girl and they will
> cruise around and go down one of the dark streets, and five
> minutes later the girl will be back on the street."

It is the activity on the streets which is the problem for everyone involved, and the police are adamant about the clubs not because of anything that goes on in most of the clubs, but because of the clubs' alleged links to the street:

> "I've been patrolling the Combat Zone for years. The place
> attracts a hodge-podge of people, including a lot of legitimate
> people. The problem is not necessarily inside the clubs."

The problem is on the streets. People who hate the Adult Entertainment District hate it because they feel it is the draw that attracts all the street criminals who then prey on the innocent people who want nothing to do with the Adult Entertainment District or what goes on inside those clubs. The Adult Entertainment District is thought to be the money that draws the flies, or to use the imagery of one person, the relationship between the clubs and crime is like "a magnet and a nail".

Others believe that any place that attracts crowds of curiosity seekers will attract people to prey upon them. A probation officer says:

"Are we blaming the Zone for the prostitution problem? This is a delicate and sensitive area... it can occur right outside City Hall Plaza. Do we tear down City Hall or Faneuil Hall, just because prostitutes work out of those places too? You may reduce the problem or shift it, but not eliminate it. The Zone attracts a certain element, but it doesn't create the problem."

The opinion of at least one of the proprietors of the clubs in the Adult Entertainment District sounds very similar to the opinions of most of the other businessmen in the area:

"Several years ago the street scene around here was a horror. There would be marauding gangs of teenage black women pouring out onto the streets at 1 a.m. Street problems were everywhere. We petitioned the police for more protection, and I hired private security guards for outside my club. Then the Puopolo thing happened and for the next year and a half there were police all over the place. Now, we're back to me calling 911 a lot for help. I want good police protection on the streets to make my customers feel safe coming here."

An attorney for some of the businesses in the Adult Entertainment District is adamant about his clients not being the cause of all the problems in the area:

"The real problem here is keeping the streets safe from crime in the Zone and its periphery. A major problem to the Theatre District is attacks from the street which <u>do not emanate from the Zone</u>. The <u>Proper Name</u> is not in the Zone, and neither is the <u>Proper Name</u>. The street prostitution and the street crime are something that hurts my clients as much as anyone else."

(Don't the clubs attract and create the street traffic?)

"That could be said about any entertainment in the City, the Boston Garden, or Fenway Park. The price you pay for having people attracted to an area is that at certain hours the crowd, any crowd, is preyed upon. Those types who do the preying would be there anyway, without our clubs being there."

This attorney does not deny that the Adult Entertainment District draws people who prey on patrons, but the legitimate theatres also draw people who prey on their patrons, and he feels the Adult Entertainment District clubs should not be regarded as the <u>only</u> cause of street problems in the area. This is not to say that <u>some</u> places in the Combat Zone are not regarded as meeting points and centers of prostitution, pick-pocketing, and other crimes. One of the Adult Entertainment District club owners has this to say about the other clubs in the district:

"My place is not a clip joint. It is a 'show bar'. I made the
decision that there would be a show and people would pay for
drinks to watch the show, and they would not be paying for
any other action. No prostitutes or pimps are allowed to work
in this club. My dancers are not prostitutes. Everyone
knows that Proper Name allows prostitutes to work out of their
club. That place is the biggest source of problems in the
Zone. They should close down that place. It's just a hooker
bar."

This is the same place which a major restauranteur identified and who was
earlier quoted as feeling that the police were doing an excellent job in the
area:

"The situation was worse a few years back and the police
responded to our requests. There will always be that negative
element around -- prostitution. But, as it is now, you've (the
BRA) set up a hang-out for them. A place like Proper Name
is one big prostitution set up."

The important thing in the above quote is that while this man is referring to
the Adult Entertainment District as a whole, when he says "you've set up a
hang-out for them," his example is of one specific place in the Adult
Entertainment District. We see how the problems of one place can be so
graphic that they extend to infect the other places which may or may not be
a part of the problem. This shows the way in which the image of the Adult
Entertainment District becomes as important as the reality itself.

The Image of the Combat Zone

A basic problem for residents and businessmen in the Theatre District area is
that the image of the Combat Zone is so powerful that the whole area is
defined for many people in terms of the Combat Zone. People do not want to
live in an area "on the edge of the Combat Zone".

The feeling that the Zone's image pervades the whole area lies behind much of
the promotion of the designation: "Theatre District". The importance of this
imagery is mentioned by the following businessman:

"An important thing about the area is that the Zone image is
changing -- this is critical to us. How do I know that? Just
read the newspapers. Stories now refer to 'The Theatre
District' and not to the 'Combat Zone'. This is a major step."

The image of the Zone is strong, and is an essential part of its attraction for
many people:

"The Zone's magic is that it is bizarre. Weird things are for
sale. It's hard for the Zone to be subtle, because its glitter
is its attraction."

Glitter may be one part of the image of the Zone, but danger is as much a
part of that image. For many people danger rather than being an inhibiting
factor is part of the attraction of the Zone -- it makes it more exciting and

more adventurous to go to the Zone when there is a hint of risk in the expedition. A man who has worked in social service positions in the City and suburbs for years and who is now a resident in the area says:

"Conventioneers with money won't come to Boston without the Zone as an attraction. Guys from the suburbs and factory workers bring money. They like to take a risk for the excitement."

Risks and excitement are things that police officers talk about in terms of the "curiosity factor" attracting people to the Zone. This image of the Zone is also a factor attracting some of the people who work there. A person who has worked with prostitutes has this to say:

"The prostitutes aren't the ones who are responsible for a lot of crime. They are victims of crimes, since they're robbed, beaten by johns, and even robbed by the cops. Many women are pushed into it because they don't have the skill or education for other jobs. Prostitution is a job; it's work. Most of the prostitutes, although they haven't really thought about it, would say that they liked their jobs. They like the excitement attached to it -- new men, the aura of the Combat Zone, and its lifestyle."

This strange attraction despite possible victimization which prostitutes may experience is, thus, similar to the attraction and danger which draws customers to the Adult Entertainment District.

The image of the Zone remains strong, and in many ways overpowers any image of a theatre district. Once again, this is due in large part to the lack of image, coherence, excitement or vitality coming out of the Theatre District. The Combat Zone is the dominant image in the area as much by default as by design.

TRAFFIC AND PARKING

Although the topics of the Combat Zone and safety in the area are very volatile and emotional, the mundane topics of traffic and parking consume an enormous amount of time and attention. Whole organizations have arisen around traffic issues.

Concerns about parking link together businessmen as diverse as the huge downtown department stores, the theatres, the Adult Entertainment District clubs, and the hospital. One merchant says:

"It's true that there is traffic congestion now, but that's necessary for progress. We can't let some things get in the way, such as Bay Village's concern about cars. I can't see a Theatre District without traffic. Our audience is suburban and we'll never take the "T" here. So dealing with the cars is our biggest problem. If you discourage cars you'll destroy the Theatre District. As it is now some developments are eliminating parking, and it will be a nightmare if more parking

is not provided. The subways just don't serve the theatre-goers.
What I'd like to see on one of the present vacant lots is a big,
beautiful parking garage."

The battle over parking is seen through these comments from a resident of
Bay Village:

"Bay Village has never been anti-theatre. Lots of people
there enjoy and support it. The traffic is no good for us,
however. We can barely find parking spots on our own streets.
The businesses want Stuart Street wider and wider, but the
ideal Theatre District is set up for pedestrians to walk about.
It should blend with the abutting neighborhoods like Chinatown
and Bay Village."

The battle line between residents and businessmen over parking is clear. It
is one of the few topics which divide people in the Theatre District rather
than unite them in their struggle with an outside foe, such as the Combat
Zone. On this issue, businesses in the Adult Entertainment District are like
the businesses in the rest of the area:

"One of my biggest problems is parking. It's not like the
North Shore clubs with all their free parking. They have that
advantage of all that parking, but I have the advantage of
this being downtown, and there's always a market downtown."

This quote could as easily be coming from a downtown department store owner
comparing his advantages with those of a suburban shopping mall as it does
from its actual speaker -- a club owner. Downtown merchants of all types
are obsessed with issues of parking and traffic flow:

"The Garages are just too expensive around here. And the
Common lot is there, but people don't park under the Common
at night because they are afraid to cross it, and they can't
use it after 10:30 in the morning because it is all filled up by
then. A shuttle bus system between the Back Bay, Downtown
and Quincy Market is needed."

For the downtown merchants, as opposed to the theatre-oriented businesses,
the use of public transportation is as important as the provisions for private
automobiles:

"We don't just need more parking, we need more use of the
"T". The rise in the parking lot prices at the Riverside lot
means that it cost $2.50 to get in here on the "T". Add to
that the safety problems on the Green and Orange Lines, and
you make coming in on public transportation punitive for
people. We need improved public transportation. We aren't
asking for a million more parking lots."

Some people feel the existing parking facilities are not being effectively
promoted or advertised. A City official feels that many of the problems about
parking are related to lack of business judgment:

"Parking is very available, and it isn't costly, but the owners
of the lots don't stay open when they should, don't make their
places secure and convenient."

Lack of security and fear in the large parking structures deter many people
from using these facilities. Some residents feel that the businesses who are
crying over the parking situation are not willing to pay for improved parking
conditions, or to subsidize their customers in the lots that are convenient:

"We people who live nearby support the theatre district revitalization, but certain things have to be dealt with, such as
the theatres subsidizing parking lot fees, by validating tickets
or providing parking in some other way. They could use
another parking garage, but they don't even have the present
parking well-signed. It is often available and people not
familiar with the area don't even know it's there."

Congestion is an important problem for Chinatown, and the resultant noise
and pollution is of concern to community health workers who feel that the
problems of noise and air pollution are not being addressed. The combination
of late night noise from the clubs and the constant noise of the Expressway
creates so many problems for parts of Chinatown that one person told us, "on
Chauncy Street, sometimes you don't bother to go to sleep at all."

In sum, for merchants in the area parking and traffic is crucial because
anything that eases movement into the area is a boon for their businesses.
Once in the area, however, cars create environmental, safety and health
problems for residents.

HOUSING

Housing stands as a critical issue for downtown Boston. Demands from
Chinatown for family and low to moderate income housing are strong. Moreover,
the type of housing and economic development being planned outside of Chinatown
will not only have important ramifications for Chinatown, but for the entire
City, and it will drastically change the social fabric of the area. This section
will deal with current assumptions and opinions about housing, and it will
briefly mention some of the projects which have or are being implemented,
while the impact of all area development will be discussed later.

Chinatown and Bay Village are established communities with their own particular
interests, and the newly expanding Washington-Tremont neighborhood is
consolidating itself and developing an identity separate from these other
downtown neighborhoods. It cannot be overly stressed that the type of
housing which gets built and even the policy of establishing housing downtown
may change the essential neutrality of the area and its social accessibility.

Although it has been recognized by many of the people we have interviewed
that the diversity of the downtown and its accessibility to all as a city and
metropolitan center must be maintained, very few have thought of the possible
effects which more residents will have in transforming a central business
district into a neighborhood. A common point of view from the business
community stresses the desire to diversify the area through mixed income
housing in order to stimulate business:

"Theatre can take care of itself. What we need are people
living, eating, and playing here. This should be the core of
Boston. With the Herald building, and the Stearns, and the
Touraine rehab there is a market for housing, but it definitely
should not all be elderly housing. You put too many of any
one type of person into an area, and it becomes less interesting, less mixed and less viable economically."

Many planners and developers take the stand that new housing will not displac
anyone since there are no residents living there. Not only does such a view
overlook the fact that there are thousands of residents in Chinatown and Bay
Village, but there are also a significant number of residents in the Washington
Tremont area above Boylston Street. More important, this position fails to
note the impact that residents, especially an homogeneous group of residents,
would have in displacing certain social patterns and social activities in the
area. The following statement typifies such an opinion concerning displacemer
and high income housing:

"There is development going on all around the Gardens--the
condos at the Ritz, they're thinking of condos on Boylston
between Arlington and Berkeley, housing on Boylston between
Arlington and Hadassah Way. This will create a ring of luxury
housing around the Public Gardens. This is good; it's not
displacing anyone.

This luxury development will put pressure on the Theatre
District for this type of housing at the Liberty Tree Building
and at Washington and Boylston. Housing should be put
there."

This notion is often backed by the idea of smothering the Combat Zone with
"unrelenting respectability" by getting a "more classy" group of people in the
area.

Many see housing as the major vehicle in diversifying the area and turning it
into a desired twenty-four hour environment. For instance, one businessman
who resides in the area told us, "We need more housing--mixed income housing
It's too deserted at night and that's because nothing happens after business
hours." Another viewpoint sees residents as a leverage in instituting changes
downtown, boosting commerce, and cleaning up, if not eliminating, the Combat
Zone:

"Anything would be better than what we have now. More
housing, more retail, townhouses, expanding Chinatown,
condos in the Little Building--all this would be good.

Look at the influence a dozen or so Bay Village residents have
had: New residents would help us be on people's fannies."

However, there are those who do not believe that housing should be a prime
concern for the central business district. They seek to maintain the neutrality
and social accessibility of the area, and assert that downtown should be
reserved for centralized human service delivery, commerce, finance, and
government. As one proponent of this view stated:

"Housing should not be the only concern for this area. Housing has always been the strength of the neighborhoods. The central city should be a place for businesses, offices, and services. Housing should be in the communities and they need more help than the central city, including the Theatre District."

Others believe that housing should not be built unless it is preceded by the type of services and amenities that would support a neighborhood. Recently there has been an increase in the number of handicapped and elderly moving into the area as a result of federal subsidies for housing specifically for this group. Disappointed over the lack of neighborhood services and safety, an active resident of 80 Mason Street, concerned over his building's proximity to the Combat Zone, poor lighting, the lack of a neighborhood police detail, and recent muggings, stated:

"Bars attract money through entertainment; and this attracts parasites. Perhaps the answer is not to have HUD housing in downtown Boston. But it's a reality: when they approved it they should have been prepared to deal with it. The Police Commissioner spoke against the location of elderly housing at this location, because of public safety problems. But people here generate business, taxes for the City, and men are employed here..."

Two blocks up from 80 Mason Street, forty new residents have moved into the renovated R.H. Stearns building -- Section 8 subsidized elderly housing -- and another hundred units will soon be filled. The Chinese Golden Age Center's project to rehabilitate the Normandy Lounge on Essex Street into twenty-eight units of elderly congregate housing looks promising, and the Quincy Tower's 161 units house the elderly (80% Chinese), while two projects soon to be started will contain a total of 260 units for the elderly. The project near Stuart, Church, and Piedmont Streets (behind the Park Plaza Hotel) is slated for 140 units and will be occupied 80-90% by Chinese, and the project at the edge of the Theatre District, next to the Hotel Bradford and the Elliot Norton Park will contain 80 to 90 units for the elderly.

Using the elderly as the pioneers of the area and the means through which more housing can be developed provokes mixed opinions. Although those spoken to favor elderly housing, many do not think that the elderly should be concentrated here nor used as the leaders in turning the area around. The common reasons are provided in the following quotations:

"The biggest problem here is that we are moving ass backwards in developing the area. They are moving the elderly in here without social services. There are no grocery stores for them.

The elderly are being moved here because that is what HUD would give money for. But that makes them guinea pigs."

"It's a mistake for elderly to be put there, because they can't deal with the problems there. The people who would move into luxury housing are younger and can handle the area."

Whether or not those moving into the luxury housing would be appreciably younger or better able to handle a mugging remains unclear, yet they, too, will need social and City services and grocery stores. An opposing pro-elderl housing view poses that the elderly, more than any other group, will be listened to in their cries for more and better police surveillance and improved public safety:

> "If there is crime there now, it won't be there after the elderly vocally complain about it. Having elderly there is probably the best thing to reduce crime for the area."

Nonetheless, it seems that the housing and neighborhood problems of the elderly are similar to those of the other neighborhoods.

A consistent complaint centered around the BRA's and City's lack of a coheren downtown plan, which thoroughly deals with the housing issues for the Washington-Tremont, Bay Village, and Chinatown-South Cove neighborhoods. Before more housing is introduced in the area, all neighborhood groups feel that the City must take a stand on the Combat Zone. If the City wishes Chinatown to expand into the Combat Zone, it is expected that the City should be more cooperative and helpful. For instance, one Chinatown housing expert discussed the City's lack of aid for the Golden Age Center's elderly housing project on the Essex Street part of the Combat Zone:

> "This project, which is a Section 202--100% financing--is in jeopardy since $75,000 is owed in back taxes on the building. They are getting no cooperation from the City. When they requested forgiveness on the back taxes so that the project could proceed in the best interests of the community and the City, the request was refused because, technically, their lawyers filed the request three weeks past the deadline."

Stated more directly by a Chinatown agency director:

> "The housing plan as directed by the BRA is a shambles. In the very near future, we are going to have to know where they are going to allow us to put housing. Where are they going to put housing?"

It is also felt that the Mayor's Office of Housing is more concerned with commercial development and hence is encouraging market rate housing in the core of the downtown. Chinatown, more than any other downtown neighborhood, especially since the large influx of Chinese and Southeast Asians into Boston, is in dire need of low to moderate income family housing. As one respondent stated:

> "We need Section 8 housing, plus market housing, plus shops. the City would say no Section 8, all market."

Bay Village residents have expressed a similar concern about the BRA, one active resident saying, "The BRA is oriented toward business development and not the redevelopment of neighborhoods."

Since Bay Village, as described by one of our respondents, seeks a "no growth policy" in terms of new construction, it is more concerned with neighborhood development and participation in the planning process. They consider themselves long-term residents, and as such they wish to protect their interests as homeowners and stable renters. As one member of the Bay Village Neighborhood Association explained it:

> "We want input, and our goals are compatible with those of the theatre owners. It is the manner in which things get done that we are criticizing. We have a longer range view than do many of them. We're in for the long run.
>
> We don't want it to become a place where people go to dinner and raise hell. We need the area around the theatres, <u>our</u> area, not becoming a 42nd Street. There are plenty of bars around here already. Pushing these sorts of uses would lead to a short-sighted killing that will let the area run down again."

The common quip is that, "We don't want another Quincy Market." To them Quincy Market is antithetical to a family centered neighborhood and they don't want their neighborhood turned into another perception of Quincy Market -- "a middle class swinging singles hangout because of all those bars there."

With rents rising and condominium conversions occurring in Bay Village, residents are aware of the homogenization of the neighborhood. According to our respondents, condo conversion is less of a threat to the diversity of the area than the shortage of housing in general and its effect on rents. Although most Bay Village residents are concerned about condo conversion, one stating that, "It would homogenize the mix that is now here and which makes Bay Village so nice," others feel it is of some benefit to the community for two reasons. First, they claim that some of the worst buildings which are owned by absentee landlords would improve the area if they were converted into condominiums. Second, they claim that some of the condominiums, such as in the converted Abe Lincoln School, have not displaced anyone, but have created new housing. As discussed earlier, this displacement theory is limited in its view to the extent to which it fails to recognize that an increased residential population, particularly of a high income, will set the tone of an area and lead to a displacement of activities not compatible with their lifestyle. It is the hope of Bay Village, however, to maintain some of its diversity by holding onto its elderly population. Yet, many of the elderly who tended to live at the edge of Bay Village on Isabella Street have been forced out of the area due to rising rents, tending to make Isabella Street less transient. It is the desire of the Bay Villagers that at least a few of the elderly will be able to remain as part of Bay Village by relocating in the new subsidized apartment complexes nearby.

Chinatown on the other hand suffers from a severe shortage of housing and as a result of a spot check done by the Chinese Economic Development Corporation (CEDC), one bedroom housing units are commonly crowded with ten people. Yet, according to our informants, Chinatown finds itself in a unique situation in terms of attempting to put together housing for residents due (1) to its downtown location and the associated pressure for private market rate development; (2) its lack of vacant and suitable buildings, (3) HUD regulations concerning air pollution and dwelling standards, and (4) the lack of cooperation from the City.

Although the City has suggested that Chinatown expand into the Combat Zone and into the Leather District across the Expressway, informants seek a concre commitment. As one stated:

> . "There's always a lot of speculation about what might be, but so far there hasn't been any real commitment shown. Parcels need to be identified, there needs to be a formal commitment. The BRA had mentioned in passing that Chinatown could move into the Leather District, but again there's been no commitment or tangible support for such an expansion. Which buildings? At what cost? Are subsidies going to be firmly committed? Which owners are willing to sell? Will city or federal programs and agencies push the appropriate negotiations? Boundaries have to be identified... It costs incredible amounts of money for buildings and then vast amounts to convert commercial or industrial space into housing units."

Others are increasingly pessimistic about establishing housing in Chinatown-South Cove or the Leather District, especially without the aid of the City and subsidies for low, moderate, and family housing.

Thus, with speculation occurring in the Leather District due to the South Station development and the high cost of buildings in the Combat Zone due to "the incredible cash flow generated by businesses there which quadruples the value placed on the buildings," one housing expert felt that Chinatown has no choice but to "jump the Pike" into the South End if it is to continue as a residential community. Believing that the BRA may not be aware of the financial reasons which preclude building housing anywhere but in the South End, this individual stated:

> "Rose Associates is buying up the Leather District... Architects and speculators are quietly assembling sites there. In the past year alone, prices have gone up $4.00 per square foot."

Referring now to the problems of land acquisition and relocation of commercial tenants and residents, he continued:

> "HUD allows $3,000 per square foot for land acquisition costs, but land acquisition costs in the area run between $6.00 and $8.00 per square foot, two to three times the amount that HUD is willing or able to currently allow.

> In addition, whenever federal money is used in developments, commercial tenants as well as residents must receive a relocation allowance. Commercial tenants must be paid for loss of business and they must be physically relocated. For garment industries, the sheer costs of physically moving their equipment would run between $8.00 and $9.00 per square foot. For Zone businesses loss of business alone would run another half million (dollars). So you'd have to spend at least $1M <u>before</u> any work was done to prepare the site or build."

He went on to add that most of the buildings in Chinatown are at least 40-55% occupied by garment and other businesses. Yet, although the garment industry has an artificially low rent, they provide some employment for residents, and it would be extremely unwise and unpopular within the community to bring up the idea of sending the industries away. Facing such obstacles, many believe the only solution would be to build high rises. However, due to parking, air pollution, lignt and air circulation issues the BRA will not permit tall buildings to go up in Chinatown:

> "This decision in and of itself precludes development. It is not feasible financially to build low rises. Therefore, Chinatown must be allowed to expand into the South End, and it will be then necessary that something be done by the City to lift the moratorium on subsidized housing in the South End.

> Chinatown can't go north because of Lafayette Place, can't go south because of Tufts. East, perhaps, but what about South Station and the speculators?

> Who's going to pay for relocation?"

Unless the government intervenes to make subsidized, moderate and high income housing available, as one community spokesperson put it, "Chinatown will become a socially decayed area." Many of the leaders in this community have stressed the strong communal ties to Chinatown and have stated that many Chinese who have moved to other sections of the City or to the suburbs would return if housing were developed and the community revitalized. Said one community advocate:

> "People would return if housing were available. Young professionals who are well educated wouldn't stay as it is now... A lot of immigrants who were sponsored by relatives who lived in the suburbs and have never lived in Chinatown, would like to move here if space were available. Chinatown is convenient. You don't need a car or even the "T", since you can walk nearly everywhere you want to go."

Such people see some high income housing, such as condominiums, as an asset to the community, since it will help attract the middle and upper middle class Chinese back to the community. It is also a concern that Chinatown will not become one-dimensional with the current emphasis on federal funding for elderly housing. As one respondent stated, "I don't want to see Chinatown becoming a nursing home community." He added, "It lost its intelligentsia by not building mixed income housing" and it should attempt to lure them back." In sum, both the housing demands of Chinatown and the community's desire to work out a satisfactory and comprehensive plan with the City are strong, and its housing advocates and leaders are unrelenting in the plans to diversify and strengthen Chinatown. When asked if it was possible to build housing with all the City regulations against tall buildings and residential uses in a zoned commercial area, one respondent cited an old Chinese proverb: "Whatever results are the actions of men."

Besides the housing needs of Chinatown, the needs of other groups have surfaced in our interviews. It has been suggested that the City encourage the conversion of commercial space into artists' lofts, studios, and living

quarters and that similar space be set aside for the touring artists and companies in the Theatre District. Suggestions for ideal locations for local
artists have been in the Leather District, along Boylston Street and in the
Theatre District. As a result of certain manufacturing and commercial (CARD)
programs, housing for self-employed artists who live and work in their studios
can be encouraged through greater availability of low cost financing, but this
is sure to sharpen the competition for housing. As one person remarked, the
artist can be used as a "loss leader" in order to turn the area around by
attracting other people who will upgrade the area, but their role in the area
is marked by uncertainty:

> "In the Leather District the BRA has waffled on permanent
> variances, however the Building Department let us put eight
> condos for artists into South Station. They let them in be-
> cause we covered the economics with subsidies, and the plans
> for South Station were not set yet, so the "best use for this
> area is not housing" idea wasn't there yet. It was later zoned
> for straight housing, but the BRA has not taken a firm position
> on this yet, because it is still confused about the South Station
> development. Also there are other concerns there that they're
> trying to deal with. The Chinese are squashed and they are
> very entrenched and are going to hang in tough in the Leather
> District and Combat Zone. Tufts is also a great presence. So
> there's a lot of uncertainty about the area... Developers are
> just sitting and waiting to see what happens."

Finally, moderately priced hotels for tourists and visitors should be built if
the City wishes to attract others besides the wealthy, the expense account
business person, or the conventioneer. Instead of using hotel space to
accommodate the performing artists and their touring companies, the theatres
themselves might consider converting space in the Theatre District into studios
and living quarters which they could then rent.

As stated earlier, the City's plans to revitalize the area through the development of the Theatre District with more businesses and housing will attract
more permanent and transient populations. This will only increase the amount
of activity and hopefully create a new 24-hour environment. This means that
the City will not only have to upgrade current services already available in
the area, but it will also have to meet the demands of a residential neighborhood for better services, neighborhood safety, and amenities, such as better
street lighting, open space, and neighborhood stores.

OPEN SPACE

Boston has a fairly good reputation for protecting open space within the City.
The Common and Public Garden provide congenial settings in the downtown
area during the daytime, particularly in the warmer months. Residents of the
City, workers and shoppers as well as tourists share these parks with runaway
day trippers, musicians, bag ladies, alcoholics, de-institutionalized mental
patients, roller skaters, mounted patrol, vendors, and the ubiquitous photo-

graphers. After dark the crowds diminish. The more cautious, particularly
out-of-towners and older residents, avoid walking through the parks after
dark: except at Christmas time when the park is aglow with festive holiday
lights.

Elliot Norton Park, located in the Theatre District, has tended to remain
under-utilized since it's off the major pedestrian thoroughfare. The pedestrian
mall at the Downtown Crossing serves as a convenient rest stop for shoppers
and employees of the area as well as tourists, kids, and street people, with
its crowded, pedestrian ambiance and its many benches. However, non-shoppers
are less than welcome in the Crossing. Referring to those regarded as "street
people" one respondent stated:

> "All of those people are negative additions to the neighborhood,
> and we've done the foolish thing of encouraging them by
> laying out the Crossing the way we did. We try to handle
> them by making the area uncomfortable for them. You can't
> let the shopping bag ladies sit there all day on the benches.
> Also, Snow Place, the alley from Hawley to the First National
> Bank is a natural pedestrian walking path, but now it is filled
> with bums. They are not an attraction. We have to be parochial --
> let them move someplace else. Keep them on the Common."

One suggestion for dealing with what is perceived as a "problem" by merchants
is to lay out the benches in such a way that will make it harder for these
people to stay there. They are considered a potential safety problem and it
is felt that the police are aiding in the effort to disperse "undesirable" people
from the Crossing. Street vendors are considered a serious problem in the
area, a threat to the "retail situation". Merchants around the Crossing,
seeking to protect and nurture it as a viable and profitable retail district,
consider shoppers to be the legitimate users of the benches in and around the
Crossing.

Lack of open space is a problem primarily for residents of Chinatown and
other Chinese in the metropolitan area who rely on Chinatown as their social
community. Public areas in this community all have serious drawbacks. "The
terraced playground at the Quincy School gets a terrible crosswind and is not
the sort of place that is convenient or comfortable to congregate. Pagoda
Park is between the Expressway and the Massachusetts Turnpike, so pollution,
noise and personal safety are serious problems." According to one reliable
source:

> "The community needs open space like the Downtown Crossing...
> the only places people have to gather now are in the restaurants
> and in the streets. There's great need for a traffic plan to
> assess the feasibility of closing off one of the streets to provide
> at least some open space for strolling and sitting. Maybe a
> park could be planned in conjunction with the Gates which are
> going to be put up at the entrance to Chinatown. There's
> traffic nearby, but it would still be better than Pagoda Park."

Since the most salient issues for Chinatown are housing and employment, few
people vocalize complaints about lack of open space. However, due to the

density and overcrowding in Chinatown, open space in more amenable locations than presently exist should be given serious consideration, though not at the expense of housing, sanitation, noise, air pollution and job creation.

Chinese residents work long hours in the garment and restaurant businesses so that aside from supervised trips of children fortunate enough to be in daycare programs, relatively few Chinese children or adults have the luxury or time to spend on the Common.

SANITATION

Some of the property owners in the study area have been lax in waste disposal adding to litter dropped by users of the area. Of particular concern to residents is garbage from restaurants and other businesses, schedules of City garbage removal, the lack of on-street receptacles for trash, vomit and human waste. Some businesses are chronic offenders. For example, some restaurants are careless in packaging and removal of garbage, which not only leads to strong odors from rotting garbage, but also attracts rodents.

This problem was addressed at one meeting of the Washington-Tremont Neighborhood Association where one elderly resident of 80 Mason Street complained that, "The alley is a mess... you're (businessman) part of that... the trash is awful...". The businessman replied that his business on Boylston Street kept its trash inside their building until the day it was to be picked up, adding that they even pick up trash that belongs to other businesses. "We can only do so much as a business... I speak to the offending parties all the time about this problem." Another resident was upset about the Opera Company stating, "... it's a disgrace... even on opening night their garbage was not picked up..."

Chinatown's small area, narrow sidewalks, density and number of restaurants and tourist traffic exacerbate sanitation problems within the neighborhood. Referring to the location of the Chinese American Civic Association at the end of LaGrange Street one worker said:

> "Walking down the streets can be awful... the dirt and filth
> are a health and psychological hazard... there's vomit on the
> doorsteps."

Noise and pollution pose additional problems for Chinatown residents due to the Expressway, Massachusetts Turnpike, and traffic congestion. As stated earlier, noise makes sleeping difficult for many residents. This point is emphasized by a staff member of the Chinese Health Center who linked noise pollution to disruption of sleep patterns which result in mental health problems for Chinese in the area.

Contributing to the lack of cleanliness downtown is the human excrement on sidewalks, in alleys and in the subway tunnels. The resulting sights and smells constitute a public health problem and reinforce the image of the downtown as dirty and to be avoided. The glaring lack of public restrooms affects everyone. As one man stated: "There is a need for French 'pissoirs'... public bathrooms have been eliminated in Boston. We need them. And they must be well-lighted and cleaned, like in London. They figure out how to keep them clean." The idea of public bathrooms proved to be one of the few

to receive unanimous endorsement from all the people we spoke with during
the course of our research. One respondent underscored the need by saying,
"It's a big problem for visitors... from every quarter... and will become more
serious when the bus stations move out of the area."

PUBLIC IMPROVEMENTS

Maintenance of sidewalks and street lights pose serious concerns for all residents.
For instance, elderly residents at 80 Mason Street have been waiting for
street lights on adjacent Avery Street since the building opened its doors last
November. Preliminary work was done placing the necessary equipment in the
ground but the street lights were never put in place. One resident who is
legally blind reported that he almost killed himself on what he called the
"light stumps". He attributes the lack of street lights to "a bureaucratic
tangle and problems in communication", and believes that the goal of adequate
lighting can be accomplished. Nevertheless, seven months have gone by
without completion of the street lighting and fears for personal safety, particularly at night, keep elderly residents indoors. As another resident said:

> "So many of us older people simply do not go out after dark...
> When we walk down the block between Boylston and Avery
> Streets on Tremont, it's just so dark... if the storefront
> lights were left on... or if they could light the buildings that
> are there somehow..."

Most residents are concerned primarily about basic lighting related to fear
and safety while others emphasize the aesthetic quality of new public improvements:

> "We need interesting street lighting, interesting street furni-
> ture, sidewalks with brass inlays like the ones at Haymarket."

> "Why is the Washington-Tremont area being short-changed?
> Downtown Crossing gets brick sidewalks and nice lights... and
> we get 'Campbell soup sidewalks'... and no lights... We're
> being surrounded by beautiful developments and we get left
> out... so people will think we're part of the Combat Zone and
> they won't shop here... now shoppers glance down from the
> Crossing, see the Zone and turn the other way..."

Area merchants estimate that if residents of Washington-Tremont shopped
within the neighborhood, business would increase 20-30%. The influx of new
residents may give a boost to the small businesses, but that won't happen if
people feel unsafe there. Stores and markets which are suitable to an expanding residential population are sorely needed, particularly a food store within
walking distance. According to the president of the 80 Mason Street House
Council:

> "We need a supermarket nearby... There's S.S. Pierce and
> Casey's just past Brigham's... but they're expensive, and we
> can't afford to shop there. There's a twice a week bus to
> Star Market, but a lot of people can't carry that much in each
> trip... Elder Affairs had been funding a grocery van but that
> stopped last week... with only one day's notice! And the
> Senior Shuttle van may be cut out..."

In discussing the deficiencies of residential shopping services, the situation was summarized this way, "There are no food stores, shoe repair shops, cleaners, and so forth, except in the Chinese district. A young, enterprising grocer is needed here."

Although there is a dry cleaning business on Winter Place and a shoe repair shop is scheduled to open in the Stearns Building, supermarkets remain the most immediate shopping need of the area.

HUMAN SERVICES

Downtown Boston provides unique locational advantages which have attracted a wide variety of human service organizations beyond those which directly serve people of the area. Reflecting and adding to the heterogenity of the area, the largest and most widely known of these agencies provide few, if any, direct services to residents or regulars. Rather, their clients come from all neighborhoods of the City and they tend to have key positions in service and advocacy networks citywide, and in some cases, statewide. Though it is certainly common for central offices of all sorts to be located in the core of major cities, particularly state capitals, the importance for service agencies was highlighted by many respondents. As one administrator put it:

"We have just been here one year... and we would be hard pressed to find another place with the advantages... There is sort of a 'human services row' here."

A wide variety of social service, advocacy, health, mental health and religious organizations have found the area not only advantageous, but necessary to their survival as effective service providers.

A far smaller set of organizations target services exclusively to the population of the area: residents, transients, and/or regulars. The majority of service programs, all developed within the past decade, are directed toward the most crowded, densely populated, and by far the poorest residential neighborhood, Chinatown. This includes all the Chinese who come here for services from as far away as the New Hampshire border.

Several additional programs are geared specifically to meeting the needs of transients and regulars in the area, those temporarily in difficulty and the homeless of all ages and descriptions. The data collected from service providers as well as independent advocates and critics does provide a realistic portrait of the existing "net of services" as well as some of the gaps and unravelings of that net. The concern of this report is with the human beings who are the heart of downtown Boston, whose difficulties in surviving are inextricably interwoven with the ability of the City to regenerate itself socially as well as financially.

YOUTH

Certainly the largest number of children residing in the area are concentrated in Chinatown; and, according to one respondent:

> "The working schedule of Chinese families is more difficult
> than for most working people; which is leading to the dis-
> integration of the family. Garment workers' hours are 7:00 A.M.
> to 7:00 P.M., while restaurant workers put in from 3:00 P.M.
> to 3:00 A.M. So there's no time or energy left for participat-
> ing in civic organizations, or hardly any for dealing with each
> other within the family."

Day care openings, though growing in the last decade, are in seriously short supply partly due to the influx of immigrants from Indochina. There are several good day care programs serving the community, and the children involved are fortunate since the waiting lists are long. As one woman put it:

> "Chinatown could use more day care facilities with sliding fee
> scales because with both parents working, a family often does
> not meet the low income requirements for the existing programs.
> And at the Acorn Center (associated with the Quincy Community
> School) the waiting list has more than doubled in the past
> year -- now it's close to seventy names long..."

Programs primarily through the Quincy Community School and Youth Essential Services (YES) are programs provided for older youth after school activities, help with homework and jobs, counseling, and English as a Second Language (EASL). Discussing existing staff shortages, an administrator of the YES program explained:

> "We serve over 300 kids annually with only four youth coun-
> selors. And we receive many referrals from the school depart-
> ment and teachers, but we don't have the staff available for
> following through on counseling and service provision to these
> kids. There is absolutely no one to work with the families of
> these kids. Remember that around 20,000 to 30,000 Chinese or
> other Asian people float into Chinatown for services from the
> entire metropolitan area and as far away as the New Hampshire
> border... In the school system there are hundreds of Chinese
> kids in bi-lingual programs and there's only one bi-lingual
> guidance counselor who's a floater for the entire system...
> Many programs for youth are purely recreational in nature and
> that's not nearly enough to help keep kids out of trouble and
> fails to deal directly with their problems. Such programs do
> not lead to healthy development.

The services provided for Chinese residents are similar to those designed for other adolescents active on the streets. Chinese, black or white. Chinese youth gangs are involved in drugs and prostitution as are the runaways, day-trippers from greater Boston, and hard-core street youth of all races, religions, and ethnic groups. According to.one knowledgeable source:

"Residents of Chinatown will tell you that it doesn't exist...
but girls have been pulled right out of the Zone before.
Chinese gangs are involved in the Zone, but they do not
control the drug traffic there."

Involvement of Chinese youth in the activities cited above highlight the simi
among adolescents and is by no means restricted to this group. According
one court official:

"The attraction of downtown to kids of all backgrounds and
descriptions will always be there; and if it's not there the kids
will create it. Restaurants, entertainment, Boston Garden and
the Common will always be a draw. Subway stations are
excellent grounds for youngsters to congregate. Kids will be
there is some form... Adults think they can control activities
of kids... it's so farfetched these days... you can't control
drugs; you can educate the kids, but it's controlled by them."

Boston is a mecca for kids who run away or day trip from greater Boston
neighborhoods and surrounding towns. According to someone who works in
the area:

"Place Runaway houses approximately 600 kids a year: 95%
from New England and 50% from the suburbs... 30-40% from
Boston proper. This migration of young people into the downtown area stems not so much from the desire for excitement
per se, but involves rather, a complex of family and social
dynamics which lead kids to run away or to be 'thrown away'
from their families to varying degrees. The kids are victimized
in large measure by their families, and schools, etc., both
physically and psychologically... We primarily have contact
with kids who hang out around the Commons and sometimes,
but not as often, with kids involved in the Zone... I can't
stress jobs enough. Don't build more bowling alleys. In many .
cases, the parents need jobs as much as the kids... and the
kids come in looking for excitement and money sometimes...
Problems with kids are linked to basic problems, and must be
considered in the broader context. More exotic band-aides will
not alleviate or eradicate the problems."

According to our sources only a small percentage of adolescents who hang
around downtown do so within the Combat Zone. However, the ones who do
are in the greatest danger of being victimized or led into destructive or
illegal activities. As a variety of people put it:

"Mug boys and mug girls are teenagers who pose as prostitutes
to rob johns; they pick their pockets. I think that the bus
station to the Common to the arcade on Washington Street to
the Combat Zone is the common route for those kids who get
involved in Zone activities."

"The kids who go to the Zone, at least the gay kids, and most
of the others, learn fairly quickly that that's not where it's

at... The kids downtown hang out around the bus station, and this phenomenon is no different that suburban kids hanging around shopping malls."

"Gay youth don't hang out in the Zone, but around Park Square and the Common down to Copley Square and Charles Street."

"Kids see the fancy cars, the big money and the flashy window dressing that goes with the Zone. The problem is, how do you get kids out of this?"

Though prostitution, both gay and straight, are activities adolescents become involved in, drug dealing, shoplifting and running errands also provide typical ways of making a living. One patrolman who knows the area said:

"Some kids are making $1,000 a week 'working' Filene's and Jordan's. The store security knows who they are, but can't stop them from coming into the store... they can only nab them if they see them snatching something. Prostitutes start around age 14, often getting into drug habits. They get beaten up if they don't make their quotas for the pimp; which is usually $200 a day, every day. So sometimes they steal to make up the difference."

Drug use and the need to get money to buy them was of prime concern to one detective who spoke of criminal involvement in general, not only in the downtown area:

"Kids get into drugs as do adults... then they need increasing amounts of money and this leads in turn to stealing... If the intake of booze and narcotics decreased a lot or disappeared, then crime would be cut in half."

Almost everyone we talked to who worked in any capacity with young people addressed the issue of resources and employment which might afford youth the opportunity to consider alternative lifestyles. Job training, with chances for upward mobility, decent pay and the ability to buy necessities and provide shelter for themselves are all critical concerns. Everyone agrees that young people have to be reached before they have been on the street too long and that limited options often lead them to crime and make them susceptible to pimps for recruitment. One man who works with kids who have been in trouble stated:

"The street pimp is a pragmatic psychologist providing food, clothing, and shelter. He develops a pattern of dependency, which is the point at which the kid is a goner."

Unfortuantely, there are far more pimps on the streets of the City than there are streetworkers who can offer the basic necessities to confused and frightened young people.

Bridge Over Troubled Water is the only agency reaching out to youth in the entire area while YES concentrates on Chinese youth. Safe shelter remains severely limited with Place Runaway House providing some beds. Bridge is a program providing medical and dental care, counseling, referral, and friend-ship.

Most people say more outreach workers and programs for adolescents downtown are needed. The specific design of those programs remains in some dispute though the absolute necessity for shelter, food, clothing and jobs remains a unifying theme. Outreach workers should be on the streets, because that's where the young people are. Several attempts have been made in the past to set up a youth hostel somewhere downtown but the idea never received the necessary support. Nearby residents even threatened to burn down the building. People who work with gay youth insist that separate shelters are needed for them because...:

> "There must be more clean decent houses to sleep in just for gay kids since they are often beaten up by straight kids in 'mixed' shelters. All shelters for all kids must be neutral zones which are safe, quiet, clean and where there are no sermons and social workers lecturing them."

However, those working with the juvenile court disagree:

> "Setting up separate shelters for gay kids would mean you're approving the problem. I do not support gay segregation, I would support special education that would be effective. If you segregate kids and label them 'homosexual'... it's like drinking... would you label kids 'alcoholic'? If, after a clinical evaluation, you find that a kid falls into x, y, or z category... then I'd support special treatment... But shelters are an absolute must for boys and girls. Overnight arrest detention centers are needed... there's need for a unit with 25 beds for overnight arrest and another 25 for continued cases... up to a couple of weeks... Kids who constantly run or kids that can be trusted should not be put together... Place is good for kids who come in voluntarily. Streetwise kids know every avenue available... hotlines, places to stay, etc... I'm most interested in kids who don't want or recognize the need for help; the ones you only find out about when they get into trouble... Shelters shouldn't/couldn't logistically be that far from the City for those who are involved with the court... Remember these places are temporary and there's a transportation problem with court officers getting kids in for trial dates, hearings, etc... We need more secure facilities and residential programs..."

One expert in the predication of juvenile problems stated that new trends in juvenile problems which have emerged over the years have been predicted at least two years in advance. As he said:

> "Though the prediction rate has been excellent over the years, no one listens. The prediction for the 1980's is a massive increase in suicide among adolescents: no psychiatric profession

could handle it... But preventive programs are never funded,
they never have been... My preventive program for this would
involve hypnosis; but that's not a mainstream approach and i
don't think people would listen."

The combination of, one, lack of adequate funding for social services of all
kinds; two, the negative perceptions regarding people who receive services,
and three, the vacuum in preventive programs, characterizes most programs
directed toward assisting adults as well as young people. There is for example
a gap in services to both adolescents and adults who become involved in
prostitution. Though boys and girls engage in prostitution at extremely
young ages, there has been a gross lack of attention to designing programs
specifically for them. However, all agencies dealing with youth have come
into contact with those involved in prostitution at one time or another. The
FACTS program works only with twelve to fourteen year old females who live
at home and day trip into the Zone and get arrested. They deal with thirty
girls in a program of intensive, long-term treatment and specific eligibility
criteria must be met before a girl is accepted into the program. In addition,
there is a little known minister and her husband who offer assistance to
prostitutes, but they have received no funding from any source. They
among the small handfull of service providers who actually reside in the area
and are intimately acquainted with the people and activities in and around the
Combat Zone and Theatre District. Important aspects of their work include
the fact that they are not judgmental; not do they discriminate on the basis
of age.

ADULTS

If the perception of young people downtown is a handicap to those who persist
in attempting to offer alternatives and give concrete survival assistance, the
attitude toward adults potentially in need of services in far worse. The
picture which emerges is exceedingly grim. Adults, perhaps aside from most
of the elderly, are viewed as creators of their own fates and in control of
their own lives. This view, commonly held by the general public, is also
reflected in the comments of some service providers. According to one person
from the Salvation Army:

"The sad thing is that a lot of people are aware of resources
and don't want to take advantage of them. For example, the
men at Pine Street Inn are aware of the rehabilitation and job
program offered by the Army, but don't seek the help... What
we need to do is develop a network of services for various
populations and do what we can to help... Not many hard core
denizens of the Zone acknowledge a desire to get out of that
life or Zone activities..."

The homeless men and women, the bag ladies and alcoholics prevalent in the
downtown area are of concern to many, though few agencies direct their
energies toward them. Dedicated staff and volunteers at the shelters for the
homeless do what they can to provide concrete services with a minimum of
constraints, attempting to allow people dignity. One woman working on
developing the de-institutionalization program for the Commonwealth asserted
that:

"If there's anything you should communicate to the BRA, it is
that many people just want to be left alone. It would be
intrusive to force these people into participating in any programs.
Our hope is to put them in peer groups, where they can learn
some socialization skills, receive information and referral.
What they also need is more shelter... only former mental
patients would be given services... Since the bag ladies and
many de-institutionalized people are not treatable, we should
give them the freedom of choice to be left alone."

It is estimated that the number of de-institutionalized men at Pine Street Inn
has risen dramatically in the past several years. As a worker there put it:

"We estimate that 35-40% of the men are alcoholics, while the
rest have been de-institutionalized... on a daily basis we feed
350-400 men for the evening dinner; by 6:00 our 240 beds are
taken, and we accommodate another 98-100 men who sleep on
the benches and floors... the milder cases are sent to the
Center Club, a private agency on Boylston Street which is a
private agency, and provides a support system/socialization
program, and does follow-up on clients. The more severe
cases are sent to the D Street mental health facility, where
we have clinical access for the more acute cases. Mass Rehab
also helps... The de-institutionalization program is a good
idea, but lacks the necessary transition phase to make it a
viable program... The State provided it with no budget so
that there is no seed money for halfway houses and the other
support services needed by these people."

The Bay Cove Mental Health Center also takes a "hands off" attitude toward
people on the street, de-institutionalized or otherwise. As one staffer there
told us:

"Anyone who comes into the system we have an obligation to
serve... however, if they don't come in, we don't do outreach.
The FACTS program is the only one here at the mental health
center that does outreach... there are a few people into sub-
stance abuse... There's a five day detox at Andrews House in
North Dorchester which provides aftercare, but it is not well
done. Resources are inadequate and leads to primarily custodial
care... If people don't get involved and hooked into the system,
they are on their own and don't want to be... Right now there
are discussion about which mental health center is going to
provide services to Pine Street Inn when it moves... Neither
B.U. Solomon Carter Fuller Mental Health Center or Tufts' Bay
Cove want to get stuck with Pine Street in their catchment
area. No one wants to deal with them... In-patient services
are chronically over-populated... Bay Cove will continue
serving patients from Pine Street who require readmission for
the coming year... but wants to hand over responsibility for
these clients to Solomon Carter Fuller... which is also over-
populated as far as in-patients go... Location is a problem for
halfway houses, anyway, residents fight against having them
in their neighborhoods..."

Another mental health counselor in the area noted that the staff at Bay Cove Mental Health Center, at least some of them, refer to the Common as "the day hospital" because there are so many de-instititionalized people who spend time there. A large number of people have been de-institutionalized over the years with no place to go and no after care programs. They swell the large number of homeless and distressed people living on the City's streets. Places for women have been in short supply, and the expansion of the Pine Street Inn to include beds for women is welcomed by existing facilities. Workers belive there's a double standard for homeless women:

"Women who are down and out are treated much worse than men in the same situation. There are a lot of crude social workers, who bring to their jobs a lack of sympathy and understanding and a bagfull of middle class morals. God forbid if you're an unwed mother, an alcoholic, and, even worse, a prostitute who may want to get out of the business or has been beaten up and needs a place to stay. There's much less sympathy for women... These women do get raped, mugged, and beaten up. Some seem to get victimized more than others because they look vulnerable and they never seem to learn. They don't become streetwise... And there are at least 1,000 and maybe as many as 3,000 women out in the streets... And it's getting worse with de-institutionalization and condo conversion. We've seen some elderly here (at Rosie's) who have been kicked out of their homes and have no place to go, and don't know their legal rights as renters and don't know who to turn to... They get a two week notice that they have to move out, and they're obedient: they move out because they think they have to... the number of squatters is increasing in abandoned buildings and projects like Mission Hill and Cathedral. Some of the homeless women are former suburban housewives or professional women who for some reason "snapped"... The women are less visible, sleeping in cars, and lobbies and hiding out."

The situation for adults who are residents of the downtown area is somewhat better. Conditions fall short of the desperation of the homeless. Lack of adequate income, crowding and common individual and family problems plague lower income residents. Again, these concerns are expressed most poignantly in Chinatown where the language barrier and discrimination make living in the City that much more difficult. In addition, the tide of immigrants from Mainland China and Southeast Asia assure that services of all kinds will be strained. The lack of bi-lingual and bi-cultural service programs in suburban areas and surrounding towns drive Chinese into Chinatown for services from a large geographic area. Only one or two agencies outside of Chinatown have bi-lingual staff and some of the problems arising from this gap include the following issues:

"Many people here do not report crimes... the bi-lingual hotline at CEDC will call for people but it's new and not well known yet... One woman found a drunk passed out on the sidewalk in front of her door and couldn't get in... and couldn't call anyone since she didn't speak English."

"The main problem of the Vietnamese is language. They are mostly going to school and receive welfare assistance so they don't have any problems as far as living expenses go; and this bothers some of the other residents who are scraping by working low level jobs and who aren't getting any assistance... But they need more interpreters and English language training."

"The Welfare Department has no bi-lingual workers in any offices now; people have to bring their own interpreters... bi-lingual social workers are needed. This is a possible area for training."

Services for non-Chinese adults in the area concentrate on the elderly through the Department of Elder Affairs at the State level and the City's Elderly Commission. However, aside from the elderly center on Isabella Street at the edge of Bay Village, little has been provided for the newer elderly residents at 80 Mason Street and the Stearns Building. Some have attributed this to disorganization and failures in planning on the part of DEA, the Elderly Commission, and other City departments:

"I sent a student intern to the BRA in order to develop a working relationship or liaison between the two offices. But, this person was not very helpful, and seemed confused about why the Elderly Commission had sent a representative to talk to him. Currently, staff is unavailble for outreach or advocacy through our office to help get street lighting or other things. If resources were available, the Elderly Commission could do advocacy... I wish I could do something to help..."

According to the President of the House Council at Mason Place:

"After the House Council has its first meeting, we're working on by-laws now, we'll tap into City and State resources... There are people around who are well aware of what should be made available here and how to go about getting it."

The Chinatown Golden Age Center currently provides programs for Chinese elderly. Perhaps those programs could be integrated and expanded to include the new residents, however, transportation is a serious problem.

The City's commitment to downtown revitalization must include human as well as physical development. A fully comprehensive net of social services will compliment current efforts toward physical development and job creation.

PROPOSED DEVELOPMENTS

In order to put the social situation of the Theatre District area in its proper
perspective this report must review the physical developments which have
been the impetus for much of the concern over the future of the area. In
this section we will discuss the aspects of the major developments which are
most related to the social life of the area.

Lafayette Place

Lafayette place is regarded by business people as a critical element in revitalizing the lower Washington Street area. A mixed retail-hotel-entertainment
complex, Lafayette Place's social impact will center around the people it will
draw into the area. Most businesses are excited about the boost that Lafayette
Place will give to the area. The businesses in the Washington-Tremont
Neighborhood Association have worked for a Lafayette Place design which
would facilitate a spillover of customers into lower Washington Street, while
discussions between the developers of Lafayette Place and Chinatown groups
have focused on employment opportunities in the new complex. In general,
everyone feels that Lafayette Place is the northern keystone to the development of the area and the key link between the Downtown Crossing and the
Theatre District area.

Park Plaza - State Transportation Building

The western keystone to the redeveloped Theatre District area is Park Plaza.
This development has been much more controversial than Lafayette Place, and
the present plans have been worked out with residential, business and civic
association advice. Issues such as traffic and parking, noise, building shadows,
and pedestrian access have resulted in a development which combines luxury
housing and hotels, a state office building, and retail shops.

The immediate social impact of the Park Plaza development will be greater than
Lafayette Place because the present Park Square area is the focus of much
street activity centered around the bus terminals. People and activities will
be displaced by the new development and where they will move is in debate,
although most people feel that much street activity will follow the move of the
bus stations to the South Station area. In the longer run, the Park Plaza
development will extend the luxury housing and shopping environment of the
Back Bay around the Public Garden and into the Theatre District.

In combination with the daytime street activity provided by the State
Transporation Building, the Park Plaza development will greatly increase the
number of people passing through the present Park Square area.

GSA Building

A potential development of great concern to the people interviewed is the new
federal office building planned by the General Services Administation. At the
time of this writing, the GSA Building seems to be slated for the North
Station area and will not move into the Theatre District area. Most Theatre
District interests were opposed to the GSA Building because they felt that a
one-dimensional office building would do little to enhance the around-the-clock
activity of the area. Some people, however, felt that the GSA Building,

while it was not an ideal land use, would be an improvement over what was presently in the area and would be an incentive for further development. In general, if the City can provide assurances that the Park Plaza and Lafayette Place developments will be accompanied by additional improvements in the area, the loss of the GSA building will not be mourned by business and civic groups and will be actively cheered by residential and social service organizations.

Tufts-New England Medical Center Expansion

The T-NEMC's new nutrition building will solidify its command of the area south of Stuart Street. Ecologically, Tufts' effectively seals off the Combat Zone from extending southward. Socially, Tufts' workers and patients bring a steady stream of people into the area, although it does relatively little to improve the area during the evening hours. Past periods of rancor between Tufts and the Chinese community have settled into a realization on the one side that Tufts will not disappear and on the other that the Chinese are a growing population with economic power of their own. Planning documents state that institutional expansion is not the ideal compliment to an entertainment district, and that is seen by the deadening effect which medical supply stores have on Stuart Street during the evening.

The new Orange Line MBTA stop may activate the Tufts area during the evening and provide more links between it and the Theatre District.

Theatre Renovations

The Metropolitan Center

The renovated Metropolitan Center is the focus for much of the enthusiasm within the Theatre District proper. The expansion of its stage is well underway, and with its planned program of major music, dance and other performing arts, it will have a significant impact on all other theatre activities. Issues which are of concern, however, to neighboring businesses and residents are the initial amount of rock music concerts programmed for the Center, the traffic generated by the Center, and the long range viability of the Center. These concerns focus on the workings of the Center and do not detract from the Center's role in revitalizing entertainment itself. As opposed to other developments which are tangentially related to theatre, the Metropolitan Center is a sign that theatre is a central feature of the renovated Theatre District.

The Opera House and Lower Washington Street Theatre

The Opera House is the northern counterpart of the Metropolitan Center -- an active, expanding, newly energized performing arts center. It also has some problems with its neighbors, namely issues concerning the expansion of the stage across Mason Street. It is a welcome addition to the entertainment picture, but its presently limited number of nights in which it is utilized reduces its overall impact on the social life of the area. It remains to be seen how the Lafayette Place development will combine with the Opera House to energize a block which is presently deserted and threatening to many people at night.

The Opera House would have a greater social impact if the presently vacant Paramount Theatre could be re-opened for performing arts. Together with the Modern Theatre, the three houses could provide a strong focus of activity on Washington Street. The present situation of the Paramount Theatre is particularly troublesome in terms of street activity. Its long, dark, boarded-up facade is especially threatening at night and it has a debilitating influence on the entire block.

SOCIAL IMPACT OF DEVELOPMENT

A.   Impact on Diversity

This report has analyzed the Theatre District area it is facing the key issue confronting urban areas throughout the United States; is it possible to upgrade an area and improve its economic performance without restricting the access of low and moderate income people to it?   The diversity, neutrality, and social accessibility which are the strengths of the area should not be cavalierly dismissed in the rush to secure another area of the downtown for housing for the affluent and for improved commercial opportunities.   The impact of Lafayette Place, Park Plaza, the State Transportation Building and the developments projected is seen as the dawn of a new day for the Theatre District area, but many people are concerned about the broader ramifications of this development.

The immediate reaction of most social service professionals to the planned development is concern that the City wants to make the Theatre District "another Quincy Market".   They interpret Quincy Market as a showplace for the outsider and a symbol of the way in which the priorities of the City are moving away from providing services for its people:

> "The primary interests of the developers of this area seems to
> be the development of another Faneuil Hall, since that seems to
> be the image that is often conjured up.   The theatre revitalization
> is basically directed toward the needs of the affluent and the
> tourists and the needs of the non-affluent are not a concern."

This person was particularly concerned about the projected $100 a night hotel which would be part of the Park Plaza project.   Another social service provider felt that the poor of the City were constantly being moved around and pushed away from their neighborhoods to suit the wishes of the wealthy:

> "Look at what they did to the West End!   Look at the South
> End.   The trend is to push things farther and farther away
> from downtown.   Quincy Market is not for Boston residents.
> If the Theatre District is important only because the opera is
> here and patrons who don't live in the City aren't comfortable
> coming here, I say 'tough shit'."

The antagonism expressed in this last remark is an undercurrent throughout the Theatre District area.   It is held not just by social service providers who are concerned with keeping this section of the City open to people of all social classes, but also by residents and small businessmen of the area who feel that plans are proceeding without regard for the interests of the people who have lived and worked in this area for years.   One small merchant has this to say:

> "My main concern is that the people with businesses on the
> street, who have their blood, sweat and guts on the street,
> should have a preference in what is going on here.   Do you
> think that transportation building will help me?   Bullshit.
> They are going to have outside franchises in there.   How
> many people who were there at the old Quincy Market are still
> there?   Come on, you know how it operates!   A handful of
> outsiders take over the places.

What has the City done for me? The streets are filthy. The
merchants who are here on the street are the ones who have
done everything for the area.

This is the only place left in the City of Boston with tradition,
and the outsiders will come in and steal it off of you!"

This view that big business interests and outsiders are determining the fate
of the area to the detriment of the people who have struggled and worked in
the area is captured in the remark of a person who lives in the area and who
attended a meeting of the Theatre District Organizing Committee:

"Look at all those people from the suburbs deciding what is
going to happen in my back yard!"

There are the intertwined themes that the area is going to lose much of its
diversity, and that the decisions about the area are being controlled by big
business interests. This may seem confusing to many business people because
a constant theme in their discussions of the revitalization of the area is the
need to increase its diversity:

"What we need are people living, eating and playing here.
This should be the core of Boston. There is a market for
housing here, but it definitely should not all be elderly
housing. You put too many of any one type of person into an
area, and it becomes less interesting, less mixed, less viable
economically."

Business people are confident that diversity is a key to the area:

"You can't have big blocks of huge buildings of any one type.
You need mixed use in this area. You want to have stores
with condos on the second and third floors. You want people
living in the area -- that is one of the things that vitalizes
the place. Lafayette Place will provide some activity, and you
need more mix of housing so there is a 24-hour basis of activity."

The issue surrounding diversity is clarified when it is realized that the two
groups of people are talking about very different types of diversity. For
most businessmen in the area diversity means diversity in land use, while for
most social service professionals diversity means diversity in types of people.

Business interests want a diverse mix of housing, businesses, theatres,
restaurants, offices and institutions because this mix will attract people
throughout the day and night, providing a safe environment for all the businesses in the area. The type of people that this mixed land use will attract
will be primarily affluent people with money to spend in the businesses of the
area. However, residents need not be affluent in order to achive the desired
safety of the area. Social service professionals want to see the area upgraded
also, so that it is a better climate in which to live and work. They want to
continue the diversity of land use in the area, yet not by reducing the
diversity of respectable people who are now in the area. No one is saying
the mugger and street criminal should not be controlled. What they are

- 51 -

saying is that the artists in lofts, the working family, the small merchant, the shoppers at the inexpensive stores, and the social agencies which serve the entire metropolis should not be discounted and removed.

The only indication that the Theatre District is not moving in the direction of a uniformly high rent, high style area is the elderly housing being erected there. Most people involved in development regard this housing as more of a "loss-leader" to entice more development than an indication of future directions for the area.

Just as the police view the area as basically without much of a residential population, the planners basically view it as an empty space waiting to be filled. The displacement of the activities occurring there and the area's service to the entire metropolis as a part of the downtown where one does not have to be wealthy to feel one is entitled to work, shop or play would be jeopardized by this development. The downtown of a great city cannot be increasingly restricted to just one portion of its people.

B. **Impact on Safety**

As discussed earlier, the perception of safety is related to a large degree to the image of the area rather than the true extent of criminal activities, especially violent crimes against individuals, occurring there. For instance, all businesses, whether connected to adult entertainment or not, were seriously affected by the Puopolo murder on LaGrange Street, and often bring it up as a major deterrent to people coming downtown for theatre, shopping and dining. However, with the increased residential and commercial development and the desire to turn the downtown area into an 18 or 24-hour center of activity, it is possible that the atmosphere will appear safer and less threatening with increased pedestrian activity, better lighting, and cleaner streets, while the actual number and types of crime may increase, especially without added security and police protection. There is also the possibility that some of the street activity -- male and female prostitution -- may shift from Park Square to South Station with the relocation of the bus stations, especially if these people are made to feel uncomfortable by the outcries of residents and by police crackdowns.

The anticipated increase in the numbers of residents, transients and regulars living and coming into the area should involve a re-evaluation of safety programs. In general it is felt that there may be a change from the police protection, which entails extensive street contacts and a concern with vice crimes, to the values of "consistency and visibility."

Foreseeing a decline in the Combat Zone with the rise of the Theatre District and residential neighborhoods, one public safety expert stated:

> "The revitalization will result in fewer serious crimes and more
> burglary, robbery, and larceny. There will be fewer drug
> busts and crazy things, like stopping a car and finding it
> loaded with guns. There will be fewer crimes between in-
> dividuals in the area."

Yet, there is a significant divergence of opinion concerning the impact of the Combat Zone on the residents and visitors to the area. Most would agree

that much of the crime, such as muggings and armed robbery, occur in the
late evening and early morning when the clubs close down, people are drunk
and johns get robbed, often by women posing as prostitutes. As one police
officer commented, "We often have to protect people against themselves",
suggesting that many are careless and needlessly make themselves victims.
In this respect, it is felt that residents and theatre goers will not become
victimized by the Combat Zone because it is a separate world and distinct
sphere of social activity. Theatre goers, shoppers, workers, and residents
are affected by other types of crime not linked to the Combat Zone, crimes
common in crowded central business districts, such as purse snatching and
pickpocketing, and to crimes common in neighborhoods, such as breaking and
entering. Since drugs, prostitution, and gay hustling appear to happen
wherever there are crowds of people, action, and money, it seems unlikely
that these activities will disappear from downtown Boston completely, and with
better street lighting, more residential use, and pedestrian activity, the area
may police itself.

Policing the Area

As stated earlier, more business activity, more residents and more street
activity in the Theatre District will greatly affect the policing of the area.
While many businessmen and City officials feel that it is essential to put more
economic and residential activity into the area to improve its long-term safety
in the short run there are going to be enormous problems involved in mediatih
between the old street world and the new street uses. The enormous problem
involved in pumping people into an area presently viewed as dangerous will
make increased support for the Boston Police Department absolutely essential
if they are to do their jobs.

As the police see it, the first phase of any planned commercial-residential
infusion into the area will be chaotic:

> "If you put more residents into the area at the same time that
> you still have the clubs there, that would just give them more
> victims. I don't buy the theory that residents will help the
> area. You have to deal with the problems of the area first,
> not just give them more victims. The people now in the clubs
> and bars won't change. More residents won't dilute the intent
> of these people to commit crimes, not as long as we maintain
> the existing attractions."

This officer sees all the problems coming from the clubs, but even without
accepting that premise, there is the simple fact that unless something is done
to ease the transition period, more people in the area will create more police
problems:

> "Putting more residents into this area is good, and you should
> also have more businesses. But you have to eliminate the
> cancer to do that! First, people won't move into the area if
> the Zone is still here, and second, the two things aren't
> compatible with one another -- residents and those clubs.
> And, the main thing is that if you put residents in there it
> will create a thousand-fold more problems for me! Why go all
> around the bush when you should just wipe it out?"

This police official is horrified at the problems putting people into an area that is dangerous will mean for the police force:

> "You won't get any more police there if you put more residents there -- the area is already saturated. Other areas would suffer if we put more police there."

This officer is directly refuting an assumption that is implicit in the policies of many developers and City officials. This assumption is that in order to get better police protection you have to provide more residents who will scream for better protection. The residents are used as stalking horses for other uses, because the residents have the ability to call forth police resources. As we have stated earlier, it is indeed true that the police regard the area as essentially non-residential with fewer residential complaints about illegal activities than is the case in outer neighborhoods of the City. The police do indeed respond to residential complaints in their decision to concentrate their limited resources. But it is incorrect to assume that there are sufficient police resources to meet increased residential demands for protection. There is no reason to believe that the following will actually take place:

> "If there is crime in the area now, it won't be there after the elderly vocally complain about it. Having elderly there is probably the best thing to reduce crime because their voting power can get increased police protection for the area."

The increased demand for protection does not automatically lead to its supply as stated in this response from a Police Department representative:

> "Maybe this area could be cleaned up while the clubs continue to exist if we had the numbers to police the place. But the fiscal situation is such that in the last 15 years the police force has gone from 2,800 to 1,800 cops. Unless you provide more police somebody is going to get taken if the Zone isn't wiped out when the residents come in."

Considering the controversy concerning safety downtown, it might be best to take a pro-active rather than a reactive approach to crime and public safety, and to view such a pro-active program in two phases. The first phase should correspond to a plan of action that will deal with the current transition of the area into an expanded residential base, a vibrant theatre district, and an expanded commercial area. Whereas Chinatown-South Cove and Bay Village have been the two residential neighborhoods in the area up to now, the most impacted by downtown activities, there are a growing number of residents locating here. This expanding neighborhood includes the residents at the elderly and handicapped apartments of 80 Mason Street and the R.H. Stearns Building, the residents of Tremont-on-the-Common and the Hotel Touraine, as well as the increasing numbers of artists living in lofts on the upper floors of many of the buildings downtown and in the Leather District. Also to be included in this neighborhood will be the new residents of the proposed luxury apartment/condominium complexes along the Boston Common and in the financial district, and the urban ministers who will be living in the House of Many Mansions.

Phase I, although a transitional stage marked by indeterminancy, will run more smoothly if the police and City recognize that the area will, at the minimum, maintain its present activities _and_ will take on more and more of a neighborhood atmosphere as the number of residents increase. This would suggest that the police will have to deal with the types of crimes and deviant behavior traditionally associated with the different areas of downtown, such as the central business district, the Combat Zone, Chinatown, and Bay Village and that they will be dealing with an additional set of problems related to the influx of new residents. The job of the police will be more demanding as the area becomes inundated with round-the-clock activity, which will bring in more shoppers, workers, tourists, theatre-goers, and other transients. All this increased social activity downtown should entail a greater allocation of police resources in this area or an expansion of the police department if reallocation would leave other neighborhoods without adequate police protection. Whether the costs of this police protection will be covered by the tax revenues generated in this section of the City or will result in increased taxes remains a question for the Tax Department.

The City should strongly encourage private developments to hire their own security forces. This will relieve the taxpayer and lift some of the burden from the Boston Police Department.

Phase II will occur when a new equilibrium has been established downtown, which may not be for over a decade, although a large bulk of the redevelopment plans are slated to be completed before 1985. At this point a routine should have been established, patterns of activities noted, and an efficient and effective program of policing the area instituted.

C. Impact on the Combat Zone

Development in the area will change the Zone, but there are radically different opinions regarding the direction of this change.

As was stated previously, a distinction must be made between the Adult Entertainment District's _businesses_ and the entire social and geographic street world called the Combat Zone. We will look first at how these _businesses_ will be influenced by the changes in the area.

Many people hope the Adult Entertainment District clubs will wither away. They base this view on their analysis of the effects which will have increasing land use costs and changes in client demand on the profit margins of the clubs.

The clubs, initially located in this part of the downtown because of its relatively low rents. With an increase in property values it is believed the club will operate with a smaller profit and will eventually move to areas with lower operating costs. There is an element of wishful thinking in most of these assessments, because business profits are unknown. Many people think that the clubs are presently wildly profitable but that is not the expressed opinion of at least one club owner. Expecting to make a big profit during the Bicentennial, he found instead that the Puopolo incident and resultant publicity was so detrimental that he ended up "taking a bath". When asked directly if he will be able to pay the escalating costs that this location might demand, this owner said "I think so. I'll just have to wait and see what business is like in three years when my lease comes up." It is conceivable that business could increase along with operating costs.

A change in the volume of clients is the key factor in the economic withering away of the clubs and other businesses in the area. One of the businessmen in the Theatre District has the following analysis of what might happen to the clientele of the Adult Entertainment District:

> "People like to sin, but they like to sin in obscurity and
> safety. If you make the area more visible it will lead to a rise
> in rents, but it will also become too visible for the customers.
> They will no longer be coming to a place that is hidden away
> and off the beaten track."

The area as a whole will become more populated and more visible to large segments of the metropolitan populace, but since the Adult Entertainment District itself is on the small strip of lower Washington Street which is not a passage to anyplace during the evenings, there is no reason to think that those people continuing down Washington from Downtown Crossing rather than turning westward into the Theatre District will be any more visible than they are now. The visibility argument as detractor of clients assumes there will be a diversity of building uses on the same block. There is no reason to assume this will happen. The continuation of the present segregation of clubs into a small area will enable customers to patronize the Adult Entertainment District without necessarily rubbing elbows with the people going to the theatres.

The key assumptions in many people's views of the area are:

(1) More development means more legitimate street activity.
(2) More street activity means safety.
(3) More safety continues the cycle of more development.

What will this mean for the Combat Zone? Firstly, more street activity should help the area, not hurt it. As one owner said:

> "Lafayette Place will help my business. During the construc-
> tion phase I'll have the workers taking breaks. And when the
> construction is over, anything that helps downtown helps my
> business because it brings more people here."

Secondly, the connection between street activity and safety is not automatic. It requires police protection as a leading factor in the first phase. But if it is assumed that the area will become safer, that again, should help the area. The Comabt Zone's businesses are not hurt by more safety in the area. Some of the businesses which are connected with prostitution and street crimes will be hurt if these activities decline, but the relatively straight clubs, like all other businesses, will be helped by an improvement in the safety of the area.

Finally, more development in the area may start to squeeze out the Combat Zone while the ability of the major clubs to pay higher operating costs is unclear, it remains a distinct possibility. Therefore, no immediate decline in the number of clubs located in the area is foreseen.

- 56 -

D. Impact on Traffic and Parking

One impact of the proposed physical changes of the Theatre District area is that the number of people coming into the area will increase. How to handle the increased parking and traffic is of concern to residents and businesses in the area. Many residents feel that the businesses which benefit from increase traffic flow should bear some of the burden of supporting this traffic.

In terms of social planning, the way that traffic control critically impacts on the Theatre District area is in the relative importance of public transportation versus private vehicles. The new Orange Line MBTA station will benefit the southern portion of the City of Boston, but the most problematic link in the whole public transportation picture is the Boylston Street MBTA stop at the corner of Boylston and Tremont Streets. There is a drastic need to refurbish this stop and provide more security if the increase in activity in the Theatre District is not to be accompanied by an inundation of private automobiles. In terms of image, nothing could be worse than the words "Theatre District" blazoned across the dark, dank, smelly Boylston Street "T" stop. The station does nothing to alleviate the uneasiness which people have proceding from the Common down Tremont Street. This location is critical in that it is the point where the different nodes of the Theatre District should come together in a common focus, but instead it stands as an inhibitor to the development of a unified Theatre District.

Regarding provisions for automobile traffic, it is essential that present and future parking facilities be better-lighted and more secure than are most facilities in the area. Fear of these facilities is an important inhibitor preventing women who represent a majority of the theatre-going audience from coming into the area.

E. Impact on Housing

Recent trends downtown and the lack of federal family housing subsidies for the next two and possibly three years casts a cloud of doubt over the feasible rehabilitation of existing housing, the conversion of non-residential buildings into residential uses, and the building of new housing for low to moderate income tenants. Furthermore, the building of, and proposals for luxury hotels, apartments, and condominiums overlooking the Public Garden and the Boston Common seems to have already led to inflated rents and increased condominium conversions in Back Bay, Beacon Hill, Bay Village, the South End and even Chinatown. There is also some evidence that property owners in the Combat Zone, in Chinatown, and in the Leather District are taking a "wait and see" approach, while speculators are buying up property in the Leather District as a result of the South Station development. All this, combined with the effective death of rent control in the City due to the vacancy decontrol ordinance, will probably lead to a severe shortage of low and moderate income housing not only for the downtown area, but for the City as a whole.

These tendencies and, as mentioned earlier, the lack of a housing strategy and policy for the downtown neighborhoods have been the major concerns of many of those we talked to in social service, government, and business. Said one social service provider:

"With all this development downtown and all the surrounding
neighborhoods -- South End, Back Bay, Beacon Hill, East
Boston, South Boston -- the whole City is becoming 'gentrified'.
There will be no low income housing in the City of Boston if
this keeps up... De-institutionalization and the conversion of
rooming houses into condos are the two biggest causes of
homelessness. Alcoholics and battered women are part of the
problem, but condo conversion and de-institutionalization have
come to be the primary causes of homelessness...

We need to provide good housing for those who have been
displaced and forced out of the neighborhoods surrounding
downtown, and this housing that gets built should be mixed
income. (Pause) This country should provide housing for
these people or shoot them. This sounds crazy, but is it any
less crazy to force people out of their homes and literally into
the streets to die by benign neglect?... We kill ours off slowly.
We split up families, we force people to live in overcrowded
conditions, then we decide these conditions are intolerable and
kick the people into the streets and replace their cheap housing
with housing they can't afford."

The expansion of the Chinese community also seems threatened by the institutional expansion of Tufts-New England Medical Center, the competition for
more lucrative uses of property, and City regulations concerning building
heights and parking. Indeed, one respondent commented about the Chinese
community, "I'm surprised they've survived," and another stated, "I don't
see much hope for Chinatown residents because they are not organized and
will be forced out of the area if low and moderate income housing is not
fought for." However, there exists a more optimistic, combative attitude in
Chinatown, which was thus stated by one active resident:

"Chinatown's not going to be squeezed out. It's not going to
disappear. It's healthy, but some of the codes and regulations
are going to have to change. The solution to Chinatown's
housing problem is to build upward... Tufts is willing, its
Executive Committee is willing, to explore possibilities and
communicate with the community."

According to this informant, the BRA is going to have to play a greater role
as mediator between Tufts and Chinatown because the BRA split Chinatown in
half with the Expressway and let Tufts use the little land Chinatown had left:

"The BRA has four Kings, and Tufts has three Aces with the
possibility of drawing a fourth. Chinatown's enemy is not
Tufts. The BRA, not Tufts, tore Chinatown apart. It was
Mayor Collins and Logue who are responsible for the destruc-
tion of the community... Tufts is willing to negotiate; it's
willing to give something up, but when, where, and how much
has to be worked out."

:

Whether Chinatown builds more housing or not also depends on the pressure toward commercial development. At this point in time, negotiations are unde way in delimiting the boundaries of the CARD program (Commercial Area Revitalization District) and Chinatown's inclusion can create a disincentive fc developing housing. Under this program, a single commercial establishment or a broader commercial project whose redevelopment costs are at least $200, will be able to borrow money cheaply through industrial revenue bond financ CARD cannot be used for housing (except for self-employed artists who wor and live in the same place) nor manufacturing, and unless certain stipulatior are included in the CARD area plan protecting housing and manufacturing, property owners may be inclined to convert their buildings into commercial and office space. This holds true for the Theatre District and can, therefor also affect the conversion of property into housing in this area. It will become important to monitor the CARD program for the above-mentioned reasons.

In conclusion, the prospects for housing, particularly low and moderate income housing, in the area are not good. This is due to the combination current economic conditions, cutbacks in federal subsidies, real estate specu tion, and further development plans encouraging luxury housing.

F.   Impact on Amenities

Major public improvement programs associated with development of Lafayette Place, Park Plaza and the Theatre District will significantly alter the Theatre District area. If the Washington-Tremont Neighborhood Association is succes in its efforts, this neighborhood will also see improvement. Once all the sidewalks and streetlights are in place, continuing maintenance will be the chief concern. Thinking into the future one person said:

> "You have floodlights on the buildings to focus the old archi-
> tectural details, and no one objects. But there are no specifics
> about how you are going to keep it looking pretty. Who is
> going to put up and change the lightbulbs? If we leave it up
> to the City, it won't get done..."

Questions of maintenance, along with trash removal and sanitation, are per-vasive now and will be highlighted as the number of residents, restaurants and retail stores increase over the next five to ten years.

If public restrooms are provided, cleanliness and adequate lighting must be insured. Likewise, the City must provide enough trash receptacles on the street and in the open spaces, and make sure that they are emptied frequent

Noise and pollution can be expected to increase in the area as more theatre goers, restaurant patrons and residents are attracted, along with tourists an shoppers. The new parking garage at Lafayette Place will bring even more cars into the center of the area, and particularly around Chinatown. Since the clubs seem likely to remain in the Adult Entertainment District, late nigh noise will not decrease for beleagured Chinatown residents.

Shopping services geared to the needs of an expanding residential population will eventually catch up with demand. However, if luxury apartments and condominiums predominate, there may still be a gap in the shops priced for lower income residents.

The City must be prepared to meet the demands which will arise as a result of revitalization and physical development.

G.   Impact on Social Services

If development of the area draws more residents, as is planned and hoped for the need for services will grow as well. All services are strained, under-staffed and under-funded now and there's no reason to believe that will change for residents, transients, or regulars. In fact, if new residents include families, questions of day care, recreational facilities and schools will emerge in areas where they are not currently at the top of the agenda.

Everyone who works with young people knows they will be attracted to the downtown as they always have been. As one youth worker put it:

> "If every building is torn down, you'd find pockets of young people; positive or negative reactions are not the issue... It won't disappear... it may shift in quality or character... because the attractions are here... in any large city. Kids run to the lights, action, and activity 24 hours a day... An analogy would be like if you have a bucket of water with a rubber ball in it and try to hold it down... okay?... what happens when you let it go?... it bounces right back up to the top."

> "I'm not sure if the (gay) kids will move with the bus stations or not. However, they're always popular crusing spots... and are often used as recruitment sites... Often these kids are alone, they have been kicked out of their homes and their parents disown them when they 'come out' as gay."

> "Where the kids or any street action goes depends on two basic factors: the business angle and the level of comfort... for example, how comfortable is the area to hang around? The business angle refers to how kids can make money to survive by selling drugs, hustling, or whatever."

> "If some of the action moves to South Station, one of my concerns would be the close proximity of the bus station to South Boston and the consequent possibilities of increased racial violence in that area... I don't think blacks would choose to hang around South Station; so it may divide white and black activities, with black activities remaining downtown off the Orange Line."

> "The Common and downtown will continue to be a draw, no matter what moves."

Plans for the downtown area include underground walkways, covered atria in the Transportation Building and Lafayette Place and lots of bright lights, people and activity, a densely packed and layered-use area, all connected with pedestrian walkways. Despite the fact that urban designers and others say that all areas will be carefully patrolled, it will be a natural attraction to youths and others who live on the steets. The carefully orchestrated excitment, glamour and activity should prove an ever more effective magnet for people of all ages and descriptions, including the untidy and unwanted.

Some of the transients will be moved along with the bus stations and Travel Aid will go with them, in order to serve those families and individuals with transportation problems and other woes. As a result of the move of the bus stations, street people will have one less downtown location in which to get out of the cold. They will find whatever spaces are available, most likely remaining close by:

> "Street people are a breed of people that society creates that live on the street... You can't social work them away. Physical rehabilitation will not do it either. They represent a reaction to society and will exist along with the political-economic system. They exist best in soft, warm, cozy areas rather than large, cold places. A large group live between the Zone and Park Square, white and black, it's amazing. I've seen some of the same people over the past twenty-five years... they often hang out in all night restaurants. You must be careful of trying to eradicate them like rats... niches will be found, but they are likely to be increasingly less humane as physical development expands."

Services for the elderly, including an elderly drop-in center, will become an even more pressing need since the elderly are arriving in greater numbers into the area. As more elderly units continue to be built, the State and City agencies will be forced to plan for comprehensive and accessible services for elderly residents of the area.

Finally, as development pressures escalate, many offices which currently house the agencies and organizations which provide services will face higher rents and perhaps be forced out unless some protection can be given to them If they are not able to remain, a key component of the area's diversity and neutrality will be forced out and lost.

H.   Impact on Existing Neighborhoods

CHINATOWN

Although it seems highly unlikely that Chinatown as a residential area will disappear, it is possible that its social structure will change. Politically and economically Chinatown is weak, having the lowest voter turnout and the lowest per capita income of any neighborhood in the City. Much of this is due to the language and acculturation problems associated with its growing immigrant population as U.S. immigration quotas for China have loosened and a significant number of Vietnamese refugees have located in Chinatown.

Therefore, Chinatown's weakness as a neighborhood, due to the loss of its educated professional and middle class to other areas, leaves this community vulnerable to outside forces. These social forces may push Chinatown in the direction of all other neighborhoods surrounding the downtown towards displacement of the poor and lower middle classes by higher income residents. These higher income residents need not be Chinese, and can be anyone willing and able to purchase, for example, some of the new condominiums on Beach or Tyler Streets. The likelihood of professional non-Chinese moving into the Chinatown-South Cove area becomes less remote with the Tufts-NEMC in its backyard and HUD's desire to be convinced that market rate housing would work next to the hospital.*

The City should support Chinatown in its efforts to maintain its integrity and diversity as a residential, cultural, and support community. Chinatown acts not only as a home for those who live there; it also serves as the central base for the Chinese scattered throughout Boston, Massachusetts, and New England, and it provides them with social services and the security they gain in being able to be with kin and people who share the same language and culture.

BAY VILLAGE

Economically, new developments in the area are increasing the value of housing in the Bay Village area. As rental units become more expensive there will be a decline in the diversity of the Bay Village population. Elderly housing slated for the two sites on the periphery of Bay Village will provide some mix in the area, but the likely residential composition of Bay Village will be a bifurcated population -- the upper-middle class in the center and the subsidized elderly on the periphery -- as opposed to the present more heterogeneous population.

Crime and safety will continue to be of concern to the Bay Village population, expecially if greater surveillance in the Theatre District results in the displacement of street activity into the surrounding area. This has been the usual pattern when "sweeps" of anti-prostitution campaigns have occurred in the past. If this becomes the normal situation in Bay Village, the political, legal, and citizen mobilization techniques used in the past will for a time (during Phase I of the area's development) be strained. However, since Bay Village's street problems have been caused by its proximity to other more attractive areas for criminal predation, an increase in the safety of the Theatre District should not, in the long run, increase the problems of Bay Village. Major problems are likely to hopscotch over Bay Village, but it will continue to have the problems of a residential neighborhood adjacent to downtown nightclub and entertainment spots. Therefore, there will be a continuing concern with safety by the residents of the area, but a probable decline in the prostitution related problems which emanate from the bus stations as much as from the Combat Zone.

What will definitely increase will be parking and traffic problems. Increased use of the area, especially if the Theatre District businessmen continue to stress the private automobile, will greatly increase traffic and congestion around Bay Village. Programs such as business subsidies for the available parking lots are necessary in order to have the beneficiaries of such traffic pay some price for their increased business. Better utilization of parking lots will help control congestion, but noise, traffic and other automobile problems will increase for Bay Village.

---

* As stated by HUD's Eleanor White at the May 13, 1980 meeting of the Theatre District Organizing Committee after she announced the unavailability of Section 8 subsidies for the next two to three years, and pushed the 221(d)(4) housing program for middle income market rate housing.

WASHINGTON-TREMONT NEIGHBORHOOD

The recent emergence of the Washington-Tremont area as a neighborhood is directly related to physical revitalization of downtown Boston. Though there have been a number of residents there in the past and though there have always been numerous small businesses with long-term ownership patterns, interaction, communication, and organized involvement has not existed. There was absolutely no identification of the area as a neighborhood, it was a retail area with residents concentrated in multi-unit buildings or scattered above stores and restaurants. The primary catalyst for altering the situation was the announcement of plans for the Lafayette Place development on lower Washington Street, plans which were perceived by business people along the street as effectively isolating the area. Lafayette Place, rather than helping their businesses by bringing more people past the psychological barrier at the end of the pedestrian mall at the Downtown Crossing would draw shoppers into the mall complex away from them since there was limited access onto lower Washington Street. The Washington-Tremont Neighborhood Association was formed last July to organize opposition to this perceived threat facing merchants located between Lafayette Place and the Common. ·Further impetus was given to the Washington-Tremont Neighborood Association (WTNA) by the opening of the elderly housing at 80 Mason Street, and the anticipated opening of the Stearns Building. The 131 residents in these buildings along with the residents of Tremont-on-the-Common and the Hotel Touraine combine with the scattered residents in lofts and apartments to form a residential population which WTNA asserts approaches 3,000 people. According to the Association president:

> "There are thirty-two small, 'mom & pop' businesses in the neighborhood. Many merchants had a nodding acquaintance with each other after years of owning or working in the same area, but they had no real knowledge or contact with each other... Many of them are beginning a dialogue about mutual concerns after twenty years of doing business in the area... Taxes are killing them and shoplifting takes its toll..."

In addition to the lack of access to Lafayette Place, merchants are worried about how the years of construction will affect their businesses. They ask themselves whether people will be able or willing to shop there with major construction going on across the street. Contending with the negative impact of the Combat Zone on their businesses at one end of the street, the lure of the Downtown Crossing at the other, and major construction at Lafayette Place combined with rising rents and taxes, small merchants fear for their survival.

As part of the CARD plan the Neighborhood Association membership will be eligible for commercial revitalization loans. Once these funds become available changes will begin to occur within the neighborhood as well as around it. In addition, the president of the Association recently announced that a community development corporation will be formed called the Lafayette Mall Development Corporation. Through this mechanism they hope to obtain additional funds for area businesses and develop plans for the area themselves which protect existing businesses while attracting new ones.

Plans for commercial development, theatre revitalization and additional housi
guarantee that the Washington-Tremont neighborhood will remain in a transi
phase and undergo considerable dislocation and adjustment problems within
the coming decade.

SUMMARY AND RECOMMENDATIONS

This report has tried to serve as a forum for analyzing the social consequences of development of the area of the Theatre District. A summation of the findings of this report entails two different levels of recommendations. The first level of recommendations is essentially a statement of <u>issues</u> which we have analyzed and critical <u>distinctions</u> which must be realized as this area changes. The second level of recommendations entails more specific programmatic changes designed to deal with these basic issues. These programs fit within existing resources but respond to the more critical issues which must continually be kept in mind.

Major Distinctions and Issues

1. <u>The Theatre District Area is not a vacuum to be filled.</u>

Many development plans for the area treat it as a space that is essentially empty and in need of filling. The area is most emphatically <u>not</u> empty. Developments in the area are altering a present social reality that is strong, durable and complex. The area is underdeveloped from a business point of view and is, therefore, attractive for business development, but this development will take place <u>within</u> the present social fabric.

2. <u>The Theatre District area is a part of the downtown.</u>

The downtown of any city is essentially a place of communication and exchange for the entire metropolis. To continue to act as the vital center for the metropolis the downtown must continually attract and serve the needs of all its people. There is going to be a great deal of movement, of transience, and of interaction among people who are essentially strangers to one aother. This fact makes this area's life essentially different from the social reality of outlying neighborhoods, where non-residents are infrequent visitors and within which relatively circumscribed standards of behavior can be developed and informally controlled. The downtown must deal with a broader range of styles and behaviors than would be tolerated in an outlying neighborhood. Because the Theatre District is downtown, what happens to it reverberates across the entire City and region.

3. <u>The Theatre District area is presently serving as a meeting ground for the entire population of the City.</u>

The Theatre District area has not become the special turf of any one particular social, economic, ethnic or racial group, and because of this it is one of the few parts of the City which is open to all, accessible to all, and potentially of service to all the people of the City. The rest of the downtown is increasingly becoming off-limits to people who are not affluent, are not white, and are not middle class. Because the Theatre District has hitherto been of limited attraction for large development it has become a potpourri of land uses, people and activities. <u>Rather than regarding this diversity as an unimportant or negative aspect of its economic situation, this social diversity should be highlighted as a principal attraction, strength and contribution of this area to the City as a whole.</u>

4.   Promoting the social diversity of the area is compatible with improving the economic climate of the area.

Business people are vitally concerned with new developments in the area because they want the area to be more active during the day and during the night. More activity is desired not so much because of the business that accrue directly from new office workers and residents, but more importantly, because increased street activity will encourage outsiders to come into the area for shopping and entertainment. The great majority of business people feel that anything that increases the non-criminal activity of the area will be good for their businesses. There is no demand by local businesses to elimina or displace current lower income residents or discourage non-affluent shoppe office workers, students or visitors from using the myriad services in the area. Business concern with increasing activity can be met through increasi the whole range of legitimate activities now present in the area. Promoting the diversity of the area, rather than decreasing it under the erroneous assumption that homogeneity stimulates business growth, is the strategy most beneficial to local businesses, residents, and the City as a whole.

5.   Theatre District changes will result in two different phases of developme with differing needs and problems.

Growth and increase of resident, street and business activity in the area will initially take place within the existing social framework. During this Phase I of the developments, there is likely to be friction between the new population in the area and the old street activity which has preyed upon people in the past. There is no reason to think that muggers, pickpockets and prostitutes will disappear just because the area becomes more active. It is essential that critical services, such as police protection, be augmented during this phase of development. As the area becomes more active and new residents and businesses begin to feel a commitment to the area, much of the present un-savory street activity, although not disappearing altogether, should be reduc and confronted by a new type of constructive neighborhood street life. During this Phase II period, public works, sanitation and other residential services will grow in importance. It seems evident that this area will never have the paucity of street crime that could be found in outlying neighbor-hoods. Its downtown location requires a continuing concern with safety, but this burden would no longer fall as heavily on the police as it will in the firs phase of development.

Specific Recommendations

1.   A housing policy that includes low and moderate units in new development proposals.

In spite of all the problems involved in constructing anything other than market rate housing in the area, if all the new housing slated for this area is of luxury or market rate, the character of the area will gradually change so that it is no longer accessible to the City as a whole, no longer functioning as a part of the downtown. There is a drastic need for housing by the Chinese community and mixed-income housing would promote the strengths of the area as well as increase the population and street activity desired by business interests. There is no social necessity nor justification for creating yet another part of the City which meets the desires of just the affluent portion of its population. All the economic goals of the area can be achieved within a social plan promoting housing diversity.

2. A concerted and on-going campaign against the clubs and businesses in and out of the Adult Entertainment District which are contributing to prostitution and other street crimes.

The businesses which are havens for criminal activity must be prosecuted to the fullest extent of the law. These businesses include ones outside of the boundaries of the Adult Entertainment District as well as those within the boundaries of the District. Some businesses and some street corners are known to all informed parties as centers of criminal activity. Concentration of tax, licensing, police and other enforcement agency power on these most persistent and troublesome centers is preferable to across the board reactive enforcements. This is because these centers are symbols and images of the area and their elimination would have positive impacts throughout the area over and above the benefits derived from inhibiting the particular activities involved.

There is no evidence that the businesses in the Adult Entertainment District are going to wither away and die. If the zoning establishing the Adult Entertainment District were rescinded, the length of time involved in litigation and the likely "grandfather" clauses allowing present businesses to remain would together lead to no changes in the businesses in the near future. At the same time, there is no convincing evidence that Adult Entertainment District businesses would move out of the City, as is the hope of many officials, rather than spreading into other downtown areas. De-legislation of the Adult Entertainment District is unfortunately regarded as the cure to all the problems of street crime and safety in the Theatre District area, so that recommending anything other than its elimination is to many people tantamount to promoting crime. However, when viewed in the realistic perspective of what would happen if the Adult Entertainment District were de-legislated, we believe that the greater benefits to the Theatre District area and to the City as a whole would arise from a selective and vigorous campaign against the businesses and individuals which contribute to the street crime in the area.

A campaign against the problem spots in the Combat Zone would restrict the effective influence of the Zone. Restriction of the Combat Zone rather than its elimination would permit legitimate adult-oriented businesses to remain, and would prevent the encroachment of the Combat Zone into neighboring residential and business areas. Such restriction is not easily achieved, and would require a commitment from the City to provide the funds necessary for the police and other agencies to properly do their jobs, and such efforts have already begun. This will not eliminate street crime, but it will control its most harmful manifestations.

3. A continuation of efforts to improve public transportation and parking facilities in the area.

Renovation of the Boylston Street META subway stop is critical for a number of reasons: to provide easier access into the area, to eliminate one of the prime contributors to the area's image of unsafety and physical disrepair, and to link together the diverse nodes of the Theatre District.

Publicity leading to a better utilization of existing parking facilities is important along with better ighting, signing, and security in these facilities.

Encouragement of private shuttle bus possibilities in the area is necessary.

Business subsidies for private automobile parking fees should be throughly investigated. Cost and safety, rather than unavailability of spaces, are prime inhibitors to parking lot use, and programs to alleviate these two problems should be instituted before initiating new parking garge construction.

4. <u>A need exists (a) for inter-organization cooperation among social service providers, (b) improved information and referral, (c) a special police/social service liaison training program, (d) outreach streetworkers, and (e) youth shelters and secure facilities</u>.

One of the most serious drawbacks in social service delivery downtown evidenced itself when we asked social service agencies about their links to other agencies downtown. Although the agencies dealing with similar issues were familiar with each other, most agencies tended to work in a vacuum, having no <u>formal</u> linkages or network of communication with other social service organizations. We would suggest an inter-organizational council in which all downtown agencies can faim_liarize themselves with each others' programs, establish ties for referral, and coordinate service delivery to maximize effectiveness and efficiency. Currently there does not appear to be any needless duplication of services downtown, but there is a general need for expansion and an interagency council could set priorities and minimize competition for funding new programs.

In addition, we strongly urge that an information and referral booth for those in need of social services be set up, perferably on the Common. Such a booth would direct individuals in need of help to the correct social service agency. This seems to us to be one of the most cost efficient, most easily implemented, and most useful of the recommendations for short term planning.

For individuals in need of a more active intervention and for those who might not seek out the information booth, we suggest that the police, especially those working downtown, be given special training. Such training should include familiarizing police officers with the specific social problems of the youth and adults downtown and with the specific social service programs available for these groups. We urge this, since we have noted a gap in the desire of the police to help and the information they would need to be helpful.

For those individuals who might not turn towards a police officer, such as runaway youth, various outreach programs, particularly those using streetworkers are suggested. To our knowledge, few agencies have their own streetworkers, either for budgetary reasons or a belief that the individual in need of service would somehow seek and find help.

Finally, the need for clean, safe, "no questions asked" shelters for youth are needed. If possible, either through separate facilities

CPSIA information can be obtained
at www.ICGtesting.com
Printed in the USA
BVHW041351100119
537524BV00020B/955/P